"Bridget Flood writes of her personal experience with the Incarnate Word Sisters from San Antonio. Her engaging style and reflective approach gives the reader a window into the commitment of Catholic Sisters for justice in our time. It is a faith-filled read that brings joy and self-reflection. What a gift for these chaotic times."

Sr. Simone Campbell, SSS<br />Executive Director, NETWORK

"Bridget McDermott Flood offers compelling stories of women whose choices and commitments provide essential clues to the perennial quest for a life of meaning and joy. *Blue Hole Wisdom: My Journey with the Sisters* is a beautifully narrated account of wisdom garnered through the author's encounter and accompaniment of remarkable Catholic sisters providing diverse and life-giving ministries at home and abroad."

Kerry Alys Robinson<br />Global Ambassador, Leadership Roundtable<br />Author, *Imagining Abundance: Fundraising, Philanthropy and a Spiritual Call to Service*

"These accounts of faith and service present lives deeply formed by their order, caused me to think deeply about the Incarnate Word Sisters and their legacy of service to the People of God."

Dr. Kenneth Parker
Ryan Endowed Chair for Newman Studies,
Professor of Historical Theology
Duquesne University

"Bridget McDermott Flood's spiritual memoir, *Blue Hole Wisdom: My Journey with the Sisters* is just that–a journey—and a compelling one at that—filled with historical intrigue of the Sisters of Charity of the Incarnate Word's original journey from France, to tense drama with the modern day Vatican, all told in vivid detail with stories and Flood's own personal reflections. At times both haunting and electric, poignant and bittersweet, Flood narrates her own story alongside those of the Incarnate Word Sisters, with their motherhouse in San Antonio, Texas, perched on the edge of a geyser—the Blue Hole of the title. Flood's descriptions of the individual Sister's stories reflect wisdom, humor, love, even anger—and the indelible presence of lives touched by divine spirit and driven by faith–both in the initial "calling" and in the Sister's stories lived out together in service to each other and to the greater community in hospitals, schools, orphanages, and hospices across the globe.

"This is an intimate and dynamic memoir of connection, community, faith, relationships, and courage—one that I could not put down and will return to. If you are intrigued by Catholic "women of the veil," by lives guided by spirit, faith and obedience, by finding "your other gifts," you will absolutely love Flood's tales of her own life interwoven with the stories of the Sisters she has journeyed with for decades. A compelling and impressive read."

Pamela Sampel, OblSB
Writer, Professor, Spiritual Director,
Oblate of St. Benedict

"Through memorably vivid storytelling, Bridget McDermott Flood lovingly pays tribute to the Incarnate Word Sisters who have long inspired her. Anyone seeking to enliven their own faith journey will surely be moved by these beautifully crafted profiles: women choosing to accompany their sisters and brothers on the margins, animated by a deep spirituality of finding God's presence and joy in all things and every encounter."

Elizabeth A. Donnelly
Co-founder and Preacher Coordinator
Catholic Women Preach

# Blue Hole
# Wisdom

## My Journey
### *with the* Sisters

BRIDGET McDERMOTT FLOOD

# Blue Hole Wisdom

My Journey with the Sisters
Bridget McDermott Flood

Published by Incarnate Word Foundation Press
Copyright ©2020 Bridget McDermott Flood. First Edition Published 2021.
All rights reserved.

No part of this publication may be reproduced, stored in a retrieval system, or transmitted in any form or by any means, electronic, mechanical, photocopying, recording, scanning, or otherwise, except as permitted under Section 107 or 108 of the 1976 United States Copyright Act, without the prior written permission of the Publisher. Requests to the Publisher for permission should be addressed to Permissions Department, Incarnate Word Foundation Press, iwfpress@iwfdn.org

Limit of Liability/Disclaimer of Warranty: While the publisher and author have used their best efforts in preparing this book, they make no representations or warranties with respect to the accuracy or completeness of the contents of this book and specifically disclaim any implied warranties of merchantability or fitness for a particular purpose. No warranty may be created or extended by sales representatives or written sales materials. The advice and strategies contained herein may not be suitable for your situation. You should consult with a professional where appropriate. Neither the publisher nor author shall be liable for any loss of profit or any other commercial damages, including but not limited to special, incidental, consequential, or other damages.

Editor: Amelia C. Flood
Cover Art: Carolyn Flood
Cover Design: Wendy Barnes
Project Management and Book Design: DavisCreative.com

Publisher's Cataloging-In-Publication Data
(Prepared by The Donohue Group, Inc.)

Names: Flood, Bridget McDermott, author.

Title: Blue Hole wisdom : my journey with the Sisters / Bridget McDermott Flood.

Description: [St. Louis, Missouri] : Incarnate Word Foundation Press, [2020] | Includes bibliographical references.

Identifiers: ISBN 9781735517001 (paperback) | ISBN 9781735517018 (hardback) | ISBN 9781735517025 (ebook)

Subjects: LCSH: Flood, Bridget McDermott--Religion. | Sisters of Charity of the Incarnate Word (San Antonio, Tex.) | Spirituality--Catholic Church. | Spiritual formation--Catholic Church. | Nuns--Texas--San Antonio. | San Antonio River Watershed (Tex.) | BISAC: RELIGION / Inspirational. | RELIGION / Christianity / Catholic. | RELIGION / Spirituality.

Classification: LCC BX4469 .M34 2020 (print) | LCC BX4469 (ebook) | DDC 271.91--dc23

ATTENTION CORPORATIONS, UNIVERSITIES, COLLEGES AND PROFESSIONAL ORGANIZATIONS: Quantity discounts are available on bulk purchases of this book for educational, gift purposes, or as premiums for increasing magazine subscriptions or renewals. Special books or book excerpts can also be created to fit specific needs. For information, please contact Incarnate Word Foundation Press, iwfpress@iwfdn.org

MESSENGER from the volume THIRST by Mary Oliver, published by Beacon Press, Boston Copyright © 2004 by Mary Oliver, used herewith by permission of the Charlotte Sheedy Literary Agency, Inc.

Scripture texts in this work are taken from the New American Bible, revised edition © 2010, 1991, 1986, 1970 Confraternity of Christian Doctrine, Washington, D.C. and are used by permission of the copyright owner. All Rights Reserved. No part of the New American Bible may be reproduced in any form without permission in writing from the copyright owner.

All proceeds from the sale of this book support the charitable work of the Incarnate Word Foundation. www.incarnatewordstl.org

*A Life for God and a Heart for Others*
*Mother St. Pierre Cinquin, CCVI*

# Table of Contents

| | |
|---|---|
| Changing Habits: Blue Hole Wisdom | 1 |
| A Journey Over the Waters | 7 |
| Taking the Train: Answering the Call | 13 |
| Grace Comes When It Needs to Happen | 23 |
| *Chispa Divina*: We Are Sparks of the Divine | 31 |
| God Within: The Incarnation | 37 |
| Joy to the World | 47 |
| The Journey to Emmaus: Living the Spirit | 55 |
| Packing the Trunk: Answering the Call | 61 |
| The String and the Kite: What is God Telling You? | 65 |
| Bougainvillea: Finding the Garden | 71 |
| Chiapas: How Are You in Your Heart | 81 |
| Table Sharing: Creating Communities of Love | 85 |
| Going to Gruene: Finding Fulfillment in Relationships | 91 |
| Amazing Grace: The Journey Begins with a Blessing | 95 |
| Dancing the Circle: The Women of Mongu | 101 |
| Nalikwanda: Finding a Friend | 107 |
| RE-Barn: The Mission Lives Within | 115 |

| | |
|---|---|
| Give It to God: Believe | 119 |
| Deep Peace: The Vatican Visitation | 123 |
| Tea and Tamales: A Time to Forgive | 147 |
| Open the Tent Wide: Welcoming the Laity | 157 |
| Jeremiah Calls Me: Living a Mantra | 165 |
| Deep Waters: The Interior Life | 171 |
| Trust in God: Solidarity in Peru | 181 |
| Nuevo Chimbote: Beyond Where the Road Ends | 187 |
| Our Future: A Frontier Charism | 197 |
| Jubilee: Here I Am, Lord | 207 |
| 250 Bowls: Holding the Spirit | 215 |
| Headwaters at Incarnate Word: A Location, A Mission, A State of Mind | 223 |
| Acknowledgments | 227 |
| About the Author | 231 |

# Changing Habits: Blue Hole Wisdom

It all started with a small "help wanted" ad in the *St. Louis Post-Dispatch*. No one gets a job from an ad in the newspaper anymore. But I did. A single sentence in black and white led me to the Incarnate Word Sisters and Blue Hole Wisdom.

The Blue Hole is the pristine headwaters of the San Antonio River. It lies in the heart of the Incarnate Word Motherhouse lands, an oasis of calm in the middle of present-day San Antonio. When the Sisters came in 1869 the land was dotted with pecan trees, brush, and natural springs. The Blue Hole erupted as a geyser. Over time, the aquifer has diminished and from a distance the Blue Hole can be mistaken for a simple stone well—until you look down inside.

After a heavy rain, the water bubbles up, an emerald and lapis jewel. Pure. Small minnows swirl in its depths and the outpouring of the verdigris water melds into the dusty brown Olmos Creek as a spreading fan, rolling and teeming with life, heading toward the red bridge to feed the San Antonio River. At other times, the Blue Hole can be calm. The bubbles and ripples of the spring water dance beneath the tiny ferns hugging the stone walls and only a trickle feeds the river. Months pass when the Blue Hole is dry as Texas limestone, evaporated under the blistering San Antonio heat, the waters hidden below in an underground cavern.

For more than 150 years, the Sisters have worked, walked, and prayed here. Like the waters of the Blue Hole, their wisdom runs deep, clear, and pure. It is a wisdom derived from their Incarnational Spirituality, their belief that God is present in all things, and that God is most present in relationship.

When I tell people, "I work for Catholic Sisters," the picture that comes to mind is the Sisters of my childhood in black wool habits, soft with washing, layers held together with straight pins. With stiff white bibs and coifs, they were set apart in their perfection. Some were stern like Sr. Rose Louise, others sweet like Sr. Felicia, but all were ageless with wire pince-nez and Oxford style heels. Those omniscient, mysterious women held the fate of fifty squirming fifth graders dangling from a taut black cotton thread. Being "called into the office" would leave our fathers and mothers nodding in quick agreement with Sister on whatever offense had occurred. The Sisters walked with silent footsteps, separate from us all.

One Sunday each month, we'd visit Sr. Mary Patrick, my Aunt Maureen, at Mount Providence. I'd touch the white coif under the black veil to see if she still had ears. The visits in the parlor, or the courtyard during the summer to avoid the stifling heat of the motherhouse, always ended in ice cream for us, but none for her. Eating with the family was no longer allowed. She would crochet edgings onto holy cards while we had vanilla ice cream and strawberries.

The Sisters held the keys to the kingdom with a will of iron barely hidden by downcast eyes. They outnumbered the priests four to one. Founded schools and universities. Built hospitals. Managed orphanages. They taught, cooked, cleaned, and prayed. In a church and a world dominated by men, they carved out their own territory and oversaw it from sprawling Motherhouses—large Victorian brick bee-hives teeming with aspirants, novices, postulants, and those who had taken final vows. They ruled a system of nation-states–Notre Dames, Mercies, St. Joes, Precious Bloods, and the Sisters I would come to know the most, the Incarnate Words—each with their own ministries, cultures, customs, and distinctive habits. In their institutions, their word was law, and that power lingers with them still.

Then the outside world changed. In the mid-1960s, Vatican II rocked the Catholic Church to its foundations. Pope John XXIII threw open the windows, tossed out the Latin Mass for a symphony of liturgy in native tongues, and allowed the laity to step out of the pews. The black and white Church of my childhood had become a rainbow. Folk guitars replaced pipe organs. Dialogue replaced strictures. Limbo disappeared. The Sisters discerned and changed as well.

By the time I entered high school, Vatican II was in full swing and the Sisters were leaving the old habit behind. It was a shock to see Sisters in knee-length blue skirts and short veils. They not only had ears, but they also had legs. A few of the older Sisters glided down the halls in their old habits, but their numbers dwindled. Within a decade, the modified habits would be a memory too, as Sisters adapted to the dress of the day.

The symbolism of the habit has endured. Perhaps that is why the stereotypes linger, too. The habit provided the demarcation line between the sacred and the secular—the embodiment of order, authority, and certainty. It transformed the Sisters from women into a personification of Church. The backlash from leaving the habit behind was palpable. It was one thing for a Sister to have authority—quite another for that authority to be coming from a woman. This change in the Sisters was a visible manifestation of how different the Church would become and an easy target for those who were fighting to bring back the black and white Church of the past.

Not only was the habit yesterday's news: Suddenly, Sisters were no longer content to serve the Church in traditional roles. They used their discernment skills and superb management abilities to identify new calls from Vatican II's mandate of social justice and engagement with the least among us. Sisters suddenly were speaking out for the poor, leaving the schools for the streets, and visibly working with others hand-in-hand to address poverty and the public policy around it. It was quite a change from those Sisters of my childhood. Other Sisters chose a new path outside of religious life. They left the convent and went a different direction. It was a tumultuous time.

Decades later, when I started working with the Incarnate Word Sisters, I asked Sr. Cathy Vetter, CCVI, what had happened to all those wool habits. In the back of my mind I assumed each Sister had kept one hanging in the back of the closet like a great aunt's mink stole, not to be worn but to be viewed with a certain bemused nostalgia when you push the hangers aside. She smiled and told me that some of the old habits had been cut up to make the modified habits and that she had been one of the first Sisters to receive one of the new styles. This made perfect sense given that the Sisters are practical and frugal women. It was just a reflection of how rooted the stereotype was in me that I had taken for granted their love of black wool serge.

One of the sewing Sisters, Sr. Anna Vetter, CCVI, gave Sr. Cathy one of the large red embroidered scapulars that graced the front of each of the habits. Most had been burned. *Amor meus. My love.* Block letters stitched in the center of a stylized crown of thorns. She had it framed for the Foundation office, a reminder that even though styles change, the spirit remains.

Two decades have passed since I opened that newspaper. I have known the Sisters for more than twenty years. They can be wise, funny, sweet, angry, fierce, brilliant, frustrated, ordinary, and very human. Their wisdom fundamentally changed how I see the world and how I live my life. It is a wisdom that could change our world.

# A Journey Over the Waters

A letter arrives in Lyon at the Monastery of the Incarnate Word and Blessed Sacrament. Bishop Claude Dubuis, a native of Lyon now serving as the Bishop of Galveston, has written to Mother Angelique Hiver with a request that she prepare young women to serve in his diocese in Texas to care for the sick. In response, in 1867 Sr. Madeleine Chollet, CCVI, and Sr. M. Agnes Buisson, CCVI, sail from Le Havre on a ship, the Saint Laurent, to New York. From there they travel by train to New Orleans and board a second boat, the Josephine, to Galveston. A year later another young Frenchwoman, Sr. St. Pierre Cinquin, CCVI, will make the same journey.

America is coming out of a brutal Civil War, and with only a few months of preparation, these young women have left the verdant French countryside and the security of a monastic convent in Lyon for the humid seacoast of Galveston. In 1869, they continue their journey by stagecoach through the mesquite flats to San Antonio to undertake a new mission.

They arrive to find that the convent has burned, and a cholera epidemic is raging through the city. They speak French, not Spanish or English. San Antonio is a rough town, an outpost, and Bishop Dubuis is hoping these women can minister to the victims of the epidemic. Sr. Agnes leaves after two months, returning to the more established mission in Galveston.

Sr. St. Pierre and Sr. Madeleine stay with the Ursuline Sisters until a new house and infirmary are built several months later. The infirmary, Santa Rosa, is unique for its time in admitting patients no matter their race or religion. One of the first patients is African-American. They quickly establish St. Joseph Orphanage, built to serve the orphans of the epidemic.

Sr. Madeleine becomes the first superior, Sr. St. Pierre the novice director. Quiet and reserved, Mother Madeleine takes religious life seriously and follows the rule as set by the Sisters in Lyon. After three years, Mother St. Pierre takes the reins so that Mother Madeleine can work at St. Joseph Orphanage with the children, her first love. Mother St. Pierre was only in her late twenties, but she brought humor, wisdom, and a big heart to the mission, so much so that the Sisters referred to her as "Big Mama."

The Incarnate Word Sisters flourished. Less than twenty years later, Mother St. Pierre is the superior of a growing Congregation. The Sisters set their sights on

280 acres on the outskirts of San Antonio, a land of Texas scrub and abundant, bubbling springs, for a larger motherhouse. Negotiations are difficult. Colonel Brackenridge has no love for Catholics or nuns, but finally agrees to sell the land, his home and all its contents for $100,000. After the sale, he goes on a journey and when he returns, he realizes he forgot to exclude the books in his library from the sale. The Colonel asks for his books, but the Sisters keep them and have the books to this day. A deal is a deal.

The Sisters move into the Brackenridge Villa just past the geyser that is the Blue Hole. Water is abundant with streams and pooling springs nourishing oaks, cedars, willows, and cypress. Hundreds of women are drawn by the mission and a three-story motherhouse is built to house them. Many now rest beneath orderly rows of crosses behind the chapel under the spreading branches of a live oak.

The first time I went to San Antonio, I thought about those earliest French sisters. Their serene portraits hung on a wall near the chapel. And this morning they are not wise, solemn women captured behind varnish, peering through the oil pigments, but young women in their 20s who have come to a new place. The heat scorches their black wool serge habits. The geyser that was the Blue Hole must have seemed like a cool fresh miracle. Practical Frenchwomen, determined and steadfast, they encountered problems on a daily basis—cholera, fires, prejudice, and poverty. Their work quickly turned to Mexico, and Mexican women became Sisters, built schools, and created new ways to serve those most in need. The Sisters followed the Union Pacific Railroad north to Missouri and to St. Louis, setting up infirmaries and collecting change from the railroad workers on payday to cover the costs.

I thought of the Irish Sisters leaving the lush, cool valleys of Ireland and confronting a dusty olive-green landscape. The German Sisters came. Another language barrier to cross over, and the prejudice engendered by World Wars landed many of them in the kitchen as cooks, not in the classroom or the hospitals. Provinces in New Orleans and St. Louis brought Americans to the congregation. In the 1960s, the Sisters ventured to Peru in response to the call of Vatican II serving in the high Andes and becoming political targets of the *Sendero Luminoso*, the Shining Path, guerilla movement.

It all started when three young women left Galveston for San Antonio. That journey has continued for 150 years in ways they could never have imagined. And now I was part of the journey, too.

When I signed on to lead the Incarnate Word Foundation, it was new. The Sisters had sold Incarnate Word Hospital to Tenet. They had served at Incarnate Word Hospital off and on for almost a century, but times had changed. When other Catholic hospitals left the urban core for the more lucrative suburbs, our Sisters had chosen to stay with the poor, answering the original call of Bishop Claude Marie Dubuis:

*Our Lord Jesus Christ, suffering in the persons
of a multitude of the sick and infirm of every kind,
seeks relief at your hands.*

The mix of services at the hospital had dwindled. They stopped delivering babies in the 1960s. By 1997, it was known as a small inner-city hospital that served the poor and elderly with a loyal medical staff. Several Sisters remained to work in pastoral care even after the sale was complete. I went to see them, and I could tell that they were grieving the loss of the hospital. Even though it remained open under Tenet, it was not the same. We met in the cafeteria and they reminisced about the way things had been before. The medical staff was angry, and I could see that building bridges would be hard.

There had been talk about trying to raise additional funds to build the Foundation's corpus from the original $30 million that had come from the sale, but I learned that the only fundraising the Sisters had ever done at Incarnate Word Hospital was to auction a Cadillac off to the doctors every year. Given the hard feelings and lack of a donor list, there was little that could be done to augment the Foundation's endowment. And that was fine.

We would do whatever we could with the funding available. We were on the frontier of a new ministry. Compared to the other foundations in St. Louis, the Incarnate Word Foundation is a small canoe jockeying on the waves with ocean liners and schooners. Other foundations might be able to cross the ocean, but we could go up the rivers and creeks, serving the people left behind, just as the Sisters had followed the railroad nearly one hundred years ago to arrive at Incarnate Word Hospital to do the same.

# Taking the Train: Answering the Call

One question that I am frequently asked is, "Why does someone become a nun? Why would anyone want to be a Sister?"

It is easy to go with a common misconception in response. How many times have I heard or even said myself that the reason so many young women chose religious life in the 1930s, 40s and 50s was that there were limited options for women at the time? Few women had the opportunity to go to college. Becoming a Sister opened doors that were unimaginable for many women at the time. Religious life offered opportunities for education, leadership, autonomy, and security providing an alternative to the traditional path of marriage and family. Sisters could be teachers, nurses, and administrators.

Others say that women become Sisters as an escape, that it was a way to avoid dealing with problems or having to take responsibility. That being a Sister means you don't have to make decisions because you are told what to do.

Not one Sister has ever told me that any of these are the reasons she became an Incarnate Word Sister.

Choosing to become a woman religious was and remains a countercultural decision. Moreover, while some would say it is a more radical choice today, in a twenty-first century world of endless options for many young women in the United States, I would disagree after hearing the Sisters talk about why they made the choice. Embracing a call that turns your world upside down and takes you down paths you never imagined is always a radical choice, whether made in 1869, 1936, or today.

Each Sister spoke about a call.

## GOD CALLS

For Sr. Theresa McGrath, CCVI, it was God's simple call:

> *When I think about why I joined the Congregation, I didn't know a thing about the mission and the ministries. I knew a bit about Sisters because I went to school with them in Ireland, but in those days, we didn't talk much about mission and charism and I didn't come to do any particular ministry.*
>
> *I came because I felt God calling me to be a Sister. From the little I knew about Sisters, my life would have something to do with service in the Church, service to people, and just being, responding in prayer. When I came, I had no preconceived ideas of*

*what I'd be, either a teacher or a nurse. I didn't come to do a ministry.*

*I was very pleased when I was told I would go into teaching. In those days, we weren't asked what we wanted to do. I was to go into teaching and so I taught. My first assignment was to teach first grade with 65 children in San Antonio. I had just made first vows and knew nothing of American education. I was happy, however, and learned a lot!*

## Falling in Love with Love

Sr. Alice Holden, CCVI, fell in love with love:

*I never really had an attraction to religious life. I thought about being an airline flight attendant. Then I passed a strip joint on South State Street in Chicago. It was late in the evening. Pictures of mostly nude women were spotlighted outside. The 'Barker' yelled to invite me in. I remember saying, 'No, thank you,' and I kept walking to the El to take me home in Berwyn. That night, as I said my prayers, I remembered the scene and said, 'God, I wish I could do something about the position of women in the world, even if it means becoming a nun!' Then I cried, as I did not like the idea. So, I kept putting it out of my head.*

*Two years later, I was on my way to a test in Sociology—for which I had not studied! I saw a notice that Fr. X was in a certain room to see anyone thinking of religious life. Hmm...I could take the test later, after I'd studied for it. So, I went to see Father, confessing that I'd many thoughts of joining, but kept pushing them away, going to dances, etc. After a little conversation, I decided to talk with a Sister from the grade school I had attended. After that encounter, I received a letter from St. Louis with a list of what to bring with me. I needed two pair of shoes that were not fashionable. When I went to purchase them, the young man behind the shoehorn asked, 'Why are you buying black oxfords?' My honest response, 'Because I am entering the convent in a few weeks,' surprised him. He asked, 'Why are you doing that?' My immediate response surprised me, 'I guess because I fell in love with Love.'*

*That answer still surprises me and assures me that God is incarnate within me/us/ALL—yet we are often so unaware. That is the way it was and I'm more and more convinced that this life is all about LOVE... God's for us and ours for ALL...for all is God's.*

A TRAIN RIDE:

For Sr. Carol Ann Jokerst, CCVI, it was a train ride:

*I was taking the train from St. Louis to San Antonio to visit Mary Kay McKenzie and Dot Ettling who were entering the Novitiate. Alice Rothermich and Helena were on the train with me. We saw the ceremony in the chapel and visited with the new Novices. All of us had gone to Incarnate Word Academy and I didn't have a clue what Incarnational Spirituality meant. It was just words in the school song.*

*My decision to enter was a quick one. I had finished two years of college. Then two weeks to the day of that train ride I was back on the train with Alice Rothermich to return to San Antonio to enter the convent. What is strange is we hadn't talked about it. Both of us had decided we didn't tell each other. Helena entered a year later. Alice remained in the Congregation for several years and later discerned another vocation. She is now happily married and an active Incarnate Word Associate.*

*I love the word, 'Emmanuel,' God with us at all times, with all people and in all situations. I would not have made it in other Congregations. The Incarnational Christ is with us and we are Incarnational without even knowing it. The call was all about relationships. I was not thinking about becoming a nun. It was lurking within me.*

*When I made the decision to become a Sister, I already had my class schedule for that Fall, and I was concerned about my dad because my mother had passed way and I would be leaving him. I wasn't going directly back but had gotten off the train in Little Rock. I called long distance and said I wanted to enter the convent. My dad said we would talk when I got back. I took the train back to Union Station in St. Louis and my dad, aunt, and brother met me on the platform.*

*My dad handed me an envelope. In it was a letter from my pastor and a list of what I would need. That was my dad's way of saying it was okay, even though it would leave them alone since my mom had died of cancer at age 33. Two weeks later, I was back on the train. This is probably not a normal story. There were things inside of me, but they were not strong. Yet here I am 50 years later. I am so grateful to the Congregation and to my family. It has been a blessing beyond anything I could imagine.*

## RAISING MY HAND:
Sr. Mary Teresa Phelan, CCVI, raised her hand:

*At that time, Mother Florence came to Ireland and had permission to recruit women to serve in Texas. I was gearing toward becoming a Sister, but I thought, 'Which group should I enter?' I had the Presentation Sisters for day school and knew I didn't want to join them, and I was a boarder with the Mercy Sisters, but in March of 1963, Mother Florence was on one of her little tours of Ireland. She asked permission to have an assembly of girls. It was at a high school retreat and while I was in front of the Blessed Sacrament, I knew I wanted to be a Sister. The following week she came, and I raised my hand.*

*That is kind of how it was. She had photos of the Incarnate Word Sisters and everyone looked happy. Charism, I didn't know about. The novices looked happy in the photos too, and one of them was from a neighboring parish. There was a relationship there. From that day onward, I started doing what I would need to do in order to come to Texas. That was in 1964 and I was 19. I remember Mother Florence saying it was about giving your life to God and serving God by being a teacher, a social worker, or a nurse. I always wanted to be a social worker, and through teaching and working in parishes, I was able to do a lot of that work.*

A TREMENDOUS HARVEST:

For Sr. Rose Ann McDonald, CCVI, it is encapsulated in presence:

*I see myself living this call primarily by trying to be receptive to God's presence and love that permeate my existence—in nature, in events, in people. I understand my call as listening, as discerning, how God is expressing God's self in each moment of each day in all of the events and people I encounter.*

*'If I were looking for God, every event and every moment would sow, in my will, grains of God's life, that would spring up one day in a tremendous harvest.' I came across that quote in* Spiritual Illuminations, *a book by Thomas Merton, when I was a postulant. I was homesick enough to hang it up and return home to my family. This quote hit me so hard it knocked the homesickness out of me and made me*

*start pursuing another home, looking for God in all of the events and people in my life. What a call!*

SAYING GOODBYE:

For Sr. Rosa Margarita Valdés Tamez, CCVI, it meant choosing religious life instead of a married one:

*I had an aunt who was a nun and a missionary. Every one of their Sisters are missionaries. They are based in Monterrey. She told me many things about their work in Oaxaca and Chiapas, Mexico. When I was 13, one classmate told me, 'You are going to be a Religious,' but I told her I didn't want that. I wanted to get married, have children.*

*There is a saying: 'Jesus comes.' Later on, my classmate told me again. 'You are going to be a Sister.' And I said 'no,' that I wouldn't. As time went on, one part of me gradually started to want to become a Sister, while the other part said, 'No.' I was 15. I told Jesus I didn't want to be a Sister but let's leave it for a while. By the time I was 18, my heart was saying, 'Yes,' but my head was still saying, 'No.'*

*Then a boy knocked at my heart. He wanted me to be his girlfriend, and I thought, 'Yes, Lord, this is it. We might get married.' He was a great guy, very special, kind and thoughtful. At the same time, I started feeling and seeing myself in the missions. I realized I wanted to be a Sister. I was conflicted.*

*He was so good, and I didn't want to hurt his feelings. He was attending the Technológico Monterrey. They were giving him a scholarship to go one of three places—France, Italy, or Japan, and he wanted us to get married so that he could take me with him. I knew I had to tell him, but I didn't want to tell him. I started to avoid him. I decided I had to do it, but that evening he went straight to my home and went to the kitchen and talked to my father.*

*That very day, he went to take my hand and I said 'no.' I told him that I wanted to be a Sister. He was shocked. He had no idea. I was 20 years old. We had been dating for one year. I told him, 'This is what God is calling me to do. I can't do anything about that situation.' On the way home, he couldn't speak. He didn't go in when we arrived at my house—it was just me. That was the last time I saw him.*

*Many years later when I was working in Zambia, I saw a friend we had in common. I found out that he had three children. I wanted to ask how he was, but I didn't because I didn't want to start something. I didn't want to intrude.*

*Every single day I thank God for calling me to be a Sister. I feel like a fish in water.*

# Grace Comes When It Needs to Happen

When Sr. Walter Maher, CCVI, started casually chatting with me about Incarnational spirituality, the way someone else might be talking about the weather, as she was driving me to the airport after meetings in San Antonio, I realized again that working for the Sisters was not an ordinary job. So many of the conversations with the Sisters moved from casual conversations into gifted moments, opportunities to learn about presence and grace, leadership and relationship, the shift from what we are doing to how and why we do it.

Sr. Walter is one of the Irish Sisters and she possesses a beautiful spirituality. It is spirituality with a light touch and its relationship to whatever the topic might be is seamless. While she admits to being shy, Sr. Walter has a quick wit. Her genuine smile quickly puts you at ease and you immediately sense the joy and commitment she brings to her ministry, whether it is in Congregational leadership or working at the University of the Incarnate Word in San Antonio where she serves as Vice President for Mission and Ministry.

With her Irish heritage, it is no surprise that she is a gifted storyteller. The stories remind me of an Irish slip jig, nimbly moving from lighthearted laughter to quiet reflection and landing in mutual understanding. On one of my trips to San Antonio, we had a relaxing visit and Sr. Walter began the conversation by sharing her perspectives on grace and on leadership:

*I'm surprised at my life. As a youngster, I could never have imagined some of the things that I've done in my life, not necessarily because I did them, but because of the context, the community, the opportunities, and the challenges. Sometimes I was saying 'Yes,' when I really wasn't sure about wanting to say, 'Yes,' when I would have felt a lot more comfortable saying, 'No, I don't really need to say yes to that. I can wait for a while.'*

*The grace always comes at the moment when the 'yes' needs to happen.*

*I'm a little shy, and so that's been one of the great mysteries for me. Suddenly, whatever grace that I need, I have. That grace enables you to transcend or transform yourself. You allow whatever is unfolding before you to embrace you, and you flow into the experience.*

*I learned many things in my work as a younger woman that helped me in Congregational leadership. Working at the University with the international students taught me how to take risks and go forward into the experience. We had to see things in new ways that were not quite in line with the ordinary way of doing things—to step outside, look at them and move it along.*

*I had another challenge where I assumed the responsibility for the community of Sisters living at the University. In the 1980s, we made the decision to move so that the University could use our space. Many of the Sisters were elderly, and there was a whole period of chaos and craziness. We had just completed construction of The Village at Incarnate Word, our retirement center adjacent to the campus, and many of the Sisters would be moving there. We came together in a wonderful way as a community. The Sisters said, 'This is how we're going to do it,' and they facilitated the move.*

*Later, we returned for a Christmas liturgy and celebration. I used to cook a lot more than I do now, and they loved when I went into the kitchen because I could make the food very attractive and very tasty. Christmas is a special feast day for us, and that particular Christmas celebration was a coming together, a spiritual celebration of community, of transformation, and of letting go and becoming a new mystery in God.*

*Afterward, I sent a little memory book to the Sisters and some of them sent me lovely thank you notes. Sr. Josephine told me that the mystery was that no matter what was going on, I led by inviting all of them in to share the responsibilities with me. That is what leadership is for me. Everybody has a part. Everybody owns it. I am not afraid to go wash the pots. If I went into the kitchen to do the dishes, then it was an invitation for everybody else to come and participate, to come and be part of the whole. Everyone came in and it became an experience of real community.*

*In leadership, I have an utter sense of profound gratitude for everything God has given me, but also for all I received from the Sisters. Leadership is service. If there is one thing I learned through it, it's that when we open our arms and invite the Sisters in to participate, the shared leadership becomes even more powerful. When we delegate what needs to be delegated to them and the Sisters assume that responsibility, then we are on the journey together.*

As our time together ended, Sr. Walter left me with both a sense of her continuing gratitude, her belief in the power of love, and how she sees the Sisters' charism moving into the future.

*Looking back in my life, I am utterly amazed at the opportunities and experiences I have had. Out of gratitude, the heart overflows, and so I always want us to have that profound sense of gratitude to God, which is very much a part of our first Sisters. The other part is that sense of joy, the joy of the gift of life, and how I use my life to be in the presence of God in the world today. How do we use our gift of life not only as individual Sisters, but also as a community of Sisters in the world?*

*There is nothing more forceful or powerful than love. It is not just the emotional part, but love is also an intentional disciplined response. If you love someone, then you want the good of that person to be expressed. That is challenging because sometimes that means you know what's going on in a person's life and you may have to say, 'Wait a minute. I'm not sure that what you're doing right now is really what you need to be doing. Perhaps you might want to think about this.' You kind of lay it out there and you don't know if that person is going to accept or reject it.*

*If they reject it, you continue to love that person and hold that person in love, but you cannot force the act. That is very difficult to do, to stand there and hold them in love when you know that, for example, 'Kid, you're wasting 4 years of your life and not engaging the opportunity to have an education.' You have to empower yourself to not let all of that get in the way of still holding that person in love. It is not easy to do but that is the important thing.*

*We have to love just like Jesus Christ, the Incarnate Word, loved. We must also realize that at the same time He always challenged those He loved. When someone could not meet the challenge, He let him or her go, and then maybe at another point they would come back. How do we keep the heart and the space open to allow for the possibility of a conversion or change of heart? Ultimately, I believe it is about being patient with each other and ourselves, recognizing that we are all in a process that will not be completed until we travel to the next world. How do we help each other in that journey? Some days are easier, and some days are more difficult, but we should understand that we are in it together and have passion for being in it together. This is what we say our lives are about.*

*The other part of this is that we really have to know ourselves. I realize we cannot know ourselves completely, but we need to know what moves us, what un-moves us, and where we are stuck. We have to do the internal work and make the internal journey, because otherwise we are not 'real.' I think of the story of the Velveteen Rabbit, where you are pouring yourself out to others and in the pouring out you become very real. Ultimately, our life is a pouring out.*

*Some days you feel that what needs to be done here is huge and you ask, 'Do I still have the energy for that?' Even when I have limited energy, however, still there is enough of that passion. We have to know who we are and do our internal work. If we don't do that, I fear we project our own darkness, instead of light, on others. We have to be intentional and responsible about that, not only as ourselves, but also as a community gathered together.*

*As for the future, it will be a very different working style as we move from the Industrial Age of the past through the current focus on the provision of services, to a future somewhere in the Information Age, in the 'cloud.' While some work will continue, how are we going to think about where the mission is? The mission is really out with God's people. It is where they are.*

*Institutions can support the work, but more often, the mission is out there in the world. When I meet a person in the street holding a sign, I look at the person and say, 'That could be my father. That could be my mother. That could be my sister.' If that were the case, what would I want to do and how would I do it?*

*How do we stay open and how does our worldview embrace all that is going on in the world? How does it move our hearts? I find there is always a moment where the Spirit enters in. Sometimes it can be as simple as an off-hand remark that gets you thinking. Small things can begin the transformation.*

The grace always comes at the moment when the 'Yes' needs to happen.

# *Chispa Divina*:
# We Are Sparks of the Divine

On one of my trips to San Antonio, I had dinner with Sr. Alice Holden, CCVI. She had prepared all the ingredients for vegetable soup and little heaps of celery cubes, carrots, onions, and potatoes were on the counter next to the stove. A pot of broth was simmering, and Sr. Alice told me we would make our soup by dropping the vegetables into the broth after it came to boil. A little unconventional, but that is the norm for Sr. Alice.

A Chicago native, Sr. Alice is tall and angular with striking white hair and sharp features. Every conversation with her takes interesting segues. She is a poet, an artist, and to my mind, a mystic, drawing wisdom and energy from her studies of religious traditions from around the world, from nature, and from her relationships with others.

At the same time, she is committed to serving the Congregation, even when it meant putting her gifts aside and getting an MBA if that what was necessary to serve those in need. There was a lot more to Sr. Alice, however, than her credentials and service as I learned as she shared her story.

*It is amazing to me that God used me in different ways. I started as a teacher in elementary education for about 15 years and then was a principal for 3 years. Then I was asked to go to an orphanage, St. Joseph's, which I knew nothing about. It turned out that the children were not orphans – they were suffering from emotional issues. The provincial, Sr. Stephen Marie, sent me to Saint Louis University in St. Louis for 4 weeks to prepare. That is all the time I had – 4 weeks of preparation.*

*After 2 years, I was asked to go to El Paso to the children's home there and I put my foot down and said, 'No, not without a master's degree.' And that is when I went to Chicago for my MBA in personnel management. I wouldn't even be able to balance a checkbook if I had one and at least personnel management dealt with people. The Sisters never asked me to help with that again because I am too much of a free spirit to focus on that. I am off the chart with intuition.*

Since then, she has taught, worked in parish ministry, served in provincial leadership, practiced T'ai Chi Chih, and directed the spirituality center at the RE-Barn. At her essence, Sr. Alice is a creative force of nature, continually pushing boundaries. That has not been without controversy, but she owns who she is:

*My mistakes have brought me closer to God more than anything has. One of my mistakes was a wonderful art show at the Re-Barn, the spirituality center I started in our old dairy barn behind the Brackenridge Villa. When the problem occurred, I was angry as sin about it. Yet, it was such a boon when I look back at it.*

*I had organized an exhibit of paintings at the Re-Barn. The artist was handling the invitations for the opening and I didn't see those cards before they were sent, but the opening went fine. I left with a friend to go camping at the Grand Canyon. I was pretty much out of touch that entire time even though I had tried to call Sr. Blandine. I was living in a little house behind a friend's house, and when I came back, a message was tacked to the door asking that I come to the Provincialate as soon as possible.*

*I called the next morning, and oh, they were upset with me. I can't blame them, because there was a stack of faxes and letters from people around the world – the news had even made its way to an army base in Germany – about the art exhibit. There was an article about it in The New York Times. The painting the artist had chosen to illustrate the opening announcement was scandalous, to say the least. The person in Germany wrote, 'Where were you when I was growing up? I never knew a nun like you!' Others were quite harsh and said terrible things. They were scandalized. There were both extremes.*

*That was a hard time, and I learned a lot from it. The most important truth to take from that experience is that you have to be responsible for your own life. When everything hits the fan, there is nothing much you can do about it. Get out of the way if you can or lie low, but you are responsible.*

Sr. Alice shifted the conversation to spirituality, which didn't surprise me. Spirituality and the Incarnation almost always find their way into conversation with Sr. Alice:

*My life is consumed with the divine presence. It is the Incarnation. God is here within us, within everyone and sometimes we are more aware than other times.*

*Fundamentally, the Incarnation is getting in touch with our true selves who is God. I often say that when God created, he just exploded Himself. He just went boom! The Big Bang. God the Word was made flesh. The Word became the stars, the creation, everything. The Word. And the Word eventually became Jesus of Nazareth.*

*When I entered the convent to answer some of those questions, the idea of the Incarnation was Jesus of Nazareth as a 12-year-old with His little hand up, directing traffic. If you see His statue, His two fingers are up making a peace sign. After Vatican II, we examined our charism, mission, and identity. The Incarnation is not limited to Jesus of Nazareth at 12 years old. God is enfleshed in everyone. God is present in the economically poor, the emotionally poor, and the spiritually poor. God is present in all people.*

*Our response is to make ourselves aware and to spread the awareness that God is Incarnate. We work to make the actual presence of the divine credible, tangible, and audible in our world. We help people to see that God is within all of us, not a select few, or just those who are holy. That is where God is.*

*I remember when I was at St. Joseph's in Dallas and one of the Sisters said, 'What are you going to do today? You have slacks on.' (We'd just changed from the habit.) I said, 'I'm going to feed ducks.' I went to the park, fed ducks, and wrote a poem:*

*We are cold lord.*
*We are cold.*
*We are cold in our relationships with each other.*
*We are cold in ministries.*
*We are cold.*
*Blow on us and make us coals of your love.*
*We are fires of your love.*

*The idea of changing from cold to coals came in the poem. I was working with disturbed children and they would shout at us and lash out. Still, the Divine was in them, hurting – hurting terribly – emotionally, spiritually, mentally.*

*Chispa Divina – We are sparks of the Divine. We need to recognize that in ourselves, that is who we really are. That is our job, to recognize the Divine within oneself and to become who we really are. You meet yourself for the first time. We admit that the Incarnation is within each one of us.*

*It is not just Catholics or Christians that have that Incarnation, that spark. I used to think that you received this at Baptism, but that isn't it. Baptism is the celebration of your belonging to this community, this family. It is also the celebration of what is already there. The fact that you are a child of God. That we are a spark of the Divine that was always there. It is in creation. It's in the little finger. It is in the moment. It's in everywhere. What material did God have to create? When God created, there was only God. Did you ever think about that?*

We realized that several hours had passed. Sr. Alice and I returned to the kitchen to toss in the vegetables and make our soup, but the broth had boiled away entirely. We just laughed and shared bread and butter instead.

# God Within: The Incarnation

I am certain that the first—and probably last—time the words "Incarnational spirituality" appeared in the St. Louis Business Journal was in my interview about 15 years ago. From the very beginning, those words have frequently come up as part of my work at the Incarnate Word Foundation. They are the heart of the Sisters' charism, another word not usually encountered in everyday discourse that spellcheck automatically changes to "charisma." Back then, both concepts were new to me.

Charism is the easier of the two to define. Simply put, it is a special gift, Sr. Rosaleen Harold, CCVI, told me:

*Charism is a gift – not a possession. It is a gift to be shared and passed on to future generations. The Sisters do not give people our charism or pass on our charism, but as people encounter us or work with us, they discover a charism within themselves.*

*The charism comes from the spirit. People grow to recognize that in themselves.*

Charism is a gift from God that helps you live out your faith or the Gospel. In my mind, charism is the Sisters' underlying philosophy. It is what motivates them. It permeates how and why they choose to do what they do. Charism is what anchors the work of the Incarnate Word Foundation, and over time, it has become my anchor as well. That charism is the Incarnation.

*In the beginning was the Word, and the Word was with God, and the Word was God...And the Word became flesh and made his dwelling among us. John 1: 1, 14*

Incarnational spirituality sees God in us and among us. God present in our relationships with others.

At first, I kept asking the Sisters for a definition of this concept. When I would give talks about the Foundation and its mission, I was confident until I'd get to Incarnational spirituality. I was worried I'd misspeak, and that someone would ask a question I couldn't answer. I also didn't want to sound too preachy. In short, I was concerned I would get it wrong—I am no theologian by any means. Even though they could have probably put me out of my misery by giving me books to read, the Sisters didn't do that.

At the time, I found that frustrating too, but now I see the wisdom in it. I have come to believe that to understand the Incarnation in all of its aspects is impossible.

It is beyond our abilities. It is mystical. While quite a bit has been written about Incarnational spirituality, it is by living it that you begin to understand what it means to see God in yourself, in others, in your relationship with others, and in the world. The Sisters teach this concept by example, and over time, I have made connections between their actions and what is at the heart of it—living out Incarnational spirituality.

When I've asked Sisters to share their thoughts on spirituality, common threads are woven into their replies. They see Incarnational spirituality as grounded in love, in presence, in relationships, in the unique gifts within each of us.

RELATIONSHIP:

For Sr. Helena Monahan, CCVI, relationship is essential to Incarnational spirituality:

> *The divine is in every person. If I put somebody off or don't take advantage of being with that person, then I have really missed something of that person, of God and of just the experience of living. I try to live that out because it makes life calmer as every moment becomes important. I don't want to rush through life anymore. Life is not going on forever and I want to enjoy each moment as much as possible, valuing the person I am with, no matter what.*
>
> *Sometimes it is challenging to do this when you are with someone that you totally disagree with*

*on important issues. You may just want to scream because you can't imagine how they can believe what they do. That is the time to step back from your anger and realize that this is a human being who has the same reasoning and decision-making powers that I have, and that somehow they have come to this conclusion. I don't have to agree with them, and I can challenge them to the best of my ability and not become emotional. This is a huge discipline.*

*Recently I have been reading and reflecting on* Living Buddha, Living Christ *by Thich Nhat Hanh, which discusses how the tenets of the two faiths are very much alike. A key premise, and I do think it is valid, is that all of life is a continuum. There is a 'before I was born' and there is 'my life' and there is going to be 'whatever happens after I die,' but really it is all a continuum. That realization takes away fear and helps you live in the present moment without worrying about what is going to happen.*

*It is very enriching and Incarnational since 'In the Beginning was the Word, and the Word was with God.' The Word will always be. Whatever God is and whatever the Word is – the expression of God – that is what we are trying to live and that is in every person. So that is where I am.*

PRESENCE:

Sr. Kathleen Coughlin, CCVI, sees being present in our relationships as a hallmark of Incarnational spirituality:

*I would describe Incarnational spirituality as incarnating the Word in the world today and incarnating the Word in all of our interactions. For me, our spirituality is about relationships and how through those relationships the Word is brought forth. Something Sr. Sarah Lennon talked about many years ago at a presentation has stayed with me. She talked about how I listen to her when she is talking to me helps to bring forth the Word from her. And how I respond back to her is me sharing the Word from my life experiences with her. It is an enriching spiritual give and take.*

*It is very important when we are in conversation that we give that sense of listening to each other, and that comes through our body language and through where our focus is, both in terms of the person speaking and in terms of the other people in the room. If there are six of us in the room, my eye contact is not just with you. I also make eye contact with everyone to recognize that the Word is in each of us. That makes it inclusive of everyone.*

*I have tried to live that. It means quite a bit to me because I like people and I want to be in relationship with them. Putting a spiritual connotation on that experience reinforces my commitment to the Incarnate Word and the spiritual aspect of my life.*

CHRIST IN THE ORDINARY:
Sr. Annette Pezold, CCVI, sees the Incarnation as part of the fabric of daily life:

> *I would describe Incarnational spirituality as simply being able to bring Christ to my daily interactions with others. There is only one thing we need to worry about. Jesus said, 'Love your neighbor as yourself.' That to me is the real guide. Sometimes that is the only thing that gets you through, because everyone isn't always nice. It is a challenge to accept people where they are and not be judgmental, which is a common error. Once you begin to accept them, you grow and see another side of yourself.*

LOVE AND MERCY:
Sr. Rosa Margarita Valdés, CCVI, focuses on love and mercy:

> *The charism is the presence of the love of the Incarnate Word. It is a gift from God to serve this Earth, and in a special way to serve in Peru. Here I can share the mercy and the love of God with others. It is a continuing challenge for me because I will never be as big as the love of the Incarnate Word and I work to practice mercy. I continue to learn so much from*

*people in Peru and from the people I work with every day. That is living the charism.*

INTERCONNECTIVITY:

For Sr. Dot Ettling, CCVI, it is about our connectivity with others:

*As part of Incarnational spirituality, we recognize that together we are called to accept that we are brothers and sisters and that we are all responsible for each other. We are all interconnected. For me, that is the basic message of the Incarnation. Jesus came into the world as a visible sign of God's love and to say to us, there are no boundaries, it isn't they or I. It is a big WE.*

*As people, we have many boundaries and we have many barriers, but we need to break through those and truly be there for each other. Together we need to build a world, an environment, where people can thrive, where people can become who they were called to be just by the very fact of their creation, their human reality.*

*To me that is a wonderful mystery.*

PROMOTION OF HUMAN DIGNITY:

For Sr. Martha Ann Kirk, CCVI, the Incarnation encompasses human dignity:

*Here I am. Full of joy, with ever more opportunities to dwell near the heart of the compassionate One in contemplation, and ever more opportunities to try to walk with those who have less. As an Incarnate Word Sister, I need to be listening to the cries of our world. I need to be listening to the cry of creation and the cry of the immigrants. That is our vocation.*

*Our constitution says to bring the saving and healing love of the Incarnate Word through the promotion of human dignity. We are called to recognize human dignity, to promote it, to listen to the voice of the vulnerable. We are called to social justice.*

*As a teacher, I continue to think, 'What really matters? What do I want to teach?' Compassion. Social justice. Creativity. Let us listen and dwell near the compassionate heart of God. Let us be creative and know that nothing is impossible with God. Let us be risk takers and live our life with joy.*

ALIVE IN CREATION:
Sr. Theresa McGrath, CCVI, reflected on how another aspect of Incarnational spirituality is the presence of God in creation:

*I love Pierre Teilhard de Chardin, S.J. I have a card with this quote 'By virtue of Creation, and still more the Incarnation, nothing here below is profane for those who know how to see.' Earlier theology delineated a real dichotomy between the profane— the secular—and the sacred. However, when I reflect*

*Chardin's point of view, I relate that to God's presence in all of creation.*

*Everything is sacred because it is all created by God. Creation, be it persons, animal life, trees—the whole of creation is all sacred to God. So, if that's Incarnational spirituality, that God's spirit is alive, breathes, and is vibrant within every single thing then it is all sacred. It is all God's creation. To me, that is part of Incarnational spirituality. The presence of God in every, single thing. Nothing God made is bad. In Genesis, God looked on everything God had made, and it was very good. That is profound.*

*God is all around us in creation and within us. I often reflect on the Breastplate of St. Patrick:*

*Christ with me, Christ before me, Christ behind me,*
*Christ in me, Christ beneath me, Christ above me,*
*Christ on my right, Christ on my left,*
*Christ when I lie down, Christ when I sit down,*
*Christ in the heart of everyone who thinks of me,*
*Christ in the mouth of everyone who speaks of me,*
*Christ in the eye that sees me,*
*Christ in the ear that hears me.*

*Christ is within us, within everyone, and within all of Creation.*

*A MYSTERY:*

Ultimately, Sr. Brigid Marie Clarke, CCVI, describes the Incarnation as a profound mystery:

> *God, who is infinite, chose to become like us with all of our limitations, except sin. In Jesus, the Christ, the Word of God, God chose to be revealed in human form. That is profound love.*
>
> *And the revelation of who God is continues to unfold all around us in creation. The fullness of this revelation is beyond our grasp but very real. But there is more!*
>
> *The revelation of 'who God is' and 'how God is' also continues through each human being. Each of us is created to be a continuing revelation to the world of God's presence, of God's love and forgiveness and compassion, as Jesus was.*
>
> *That is who we are. What an awesome identity is ours!*

The image of the Incarnation I carry with me as a simple mantra is a quote that Sr. Brigid Marie Clarke, CCVI, shared with me at a ministry meeting:

> *Each of us is a Word of God spoken only once.*
> *— Sr. Peg Dolan, RHSM*

In the beginning was the Word, and that Word is in each of us, always present even when not acknowledged. How we bring that forth in all of its uniqueness, and how we see it in each person we meet, is the essence of who we are and what we will be.

# Joy to the World

Mornings with Sr. Dot Ettling, CCVI, and Sr. Neomi Hayes, CCVI, were always the same. Sr. Neomi rises before dawn, and since I am a late riser I am not witness to her silent steps through the house, black and white Kitty following along, brushing up against her with soft morning meows. In her 70's, Sr. Neomi is tiny, with bright blue eyes and a high-pitched Irish brogue. She spent years at what she calls, "the college," the University of the Incarnate Word, but now her primary responsibilities are writing grants and thank you notes for Women's Global Connection and providing hospitality.

Making tea, setting the breakfast table–always the blue dishes, the African placemats, the butter and jam for toast. She provides everyone with a cereal bowl even though she knows that I never eat cereal. She cuts up the fresh fruit from the counter, knowing that is my favorite. This is quite a contrast to the usual hurried yogurt smoothie I whip together on the fly when I am at home.

By the time I am up and about she and Sr. Dot are in the living room sharing their morning reflection. In her 70's as well, Sr. Dot is tall and thin with the elegant carriage of a model. She has a St. Louis accent, the same as mine, and quick brown eyes. We have similar temperaments—always doing too many things, spinning expansive ideas and creating new projects. Sr. Dot is an academic and juggles teaching, overseeing dissertations, and helping Women's Global Connection—a ministry she founded that works in Africa and South America, and fundraising.

But at morning reflection, both Sisters are at peace. Sometimes the candle is lit, sometimes not. I always pause a minute and consider Our Lady of Guadalupe in her small shrine on the table by the window; the contemporary Mexican drawing of the Visitation with Elizabeth and Mary sharing wonderful news; the Renaissance Annunciation print with Mary's small knowing smile; the African woman on the wall; the circle of terra cotta women on the table in the entrance way. All of these women, a manifestation of the power of relationship and of the divine spark within.

Whenever I come in, Sr. Neomi and Sr. Dot break their prayer and are all sunny smiles. Sr. Dot usually gives me a jovial, "Good morning, kiddo," while Sr. Neomi immediately starts fussing with tea and breakfast. A testament to her love for me is the iced tea she always has ready, even though I have an inkling that iced tea is anathema to her strong Irish soul.

When I talked with Sr. Neomi about how she lives out the Sisters' mission or charism, she began by handing me a poem by Mary Oliver that she had illustrated with drawings of hummingbirds:

*My work is loving the world.*
*Here the sunflowers, there the hummingbird—*
*equal seekers of sweetness.*
*Here the quickening yeast; there the blue plums.*
*Here the clam deep in the speckled sand.*

*Are my boots old? Is my coat torn?*
*Am I no longer young, and still half-perfect? Let me*
*keep my mind on what matters,*
*which is my work,*

*which is mostly standing still and learning to be*
*astonished.*
*The phoebe, the delphinium.*
*The sheep in the pasture, and the pasture.*
*Which is mostly rejoicing,*
*since all the ingredients are here,*

*which is gratitude, to be given a mind and a heart*
*and these body-clothes,*
*a mouth with which to give shouts of joy*
*to the moth and the wren, to the sleepy dug-up clam,*
*telling them all, over and over, how it is*
*that we live forever.*

*Messenger*
*Mary Oliver*

"My job is to bring joy to the world," she says with a crinkly-eyed smile, as matter of fact as if she were telling me the time. Then she shared her journey.

It was a journey many of our Irish sisters had taken. Leaving Ireland as a young teenager with no thought of returning. Then years spent teaching grade school, the road leading to work at the college where she listened to the hopes and cares of thousands of young women who lived in the dorms, taking a sharp turn to create a new ministry working with homeless women and their children. And Sr. Neomi's path now had turned to a life of prayer and kindness, as she tended her garden and shared her delight in the world and her sharply honed wisdom with me.

*How you see the world and your place in that world depends upon your world view.*

*I started out with a world view of fear, much different than how I see things today. I was so worried I would do things wrong. I had come from Ireland to enter the convent and in those days, you did not think you would ever go back home. My first mission was very difficult. I was at St. Frances De Sales School in New Orleans. We lived upstairs and the school was downstairs. I was only 20. After school I would sit on the merry-go-round in the playground and cry in my black habit. Did Christ ever feel that way, I wondered?*

*Over time, I developed the sense of the interior life. We would go on annual retreats and there was quite a bit of silence and time. Sundays were days of reflection. This gave a sense of discipline and perhaps in the new order of things some of this was lost. We had to pray at 5:30 a.m. When we pinned our veils, we would often draw blood because there were no mirrors, and so sometimes, I would use a window.*

*I was 3 years at the school in New Orleans, and I loved that city. We were a bit of a distance from the Congregation in San Antonio, which was nice, and then I was assigned to the college. I went to work for Sr. Antoninus, one of the sweetest sisters, who was the registrar. It must have been cruel for her those first 6 months because I did not know how to type—the mistakes I made. And so, they sent me to the Business Department and I was given 3 days to learn to type. Sr. Theresa McGrath was assigned to the Dean's office and she was so quick. I received my degree from the college in 1959.*

*As I continued at the college, I ended up living in the dormitory with the girls. I so enjoyed being with those young women from small Texas towns. I remember when* The Graduate *came out and we told them—don't go to see that with your boyfriends— and their faces would get redder and redder—how innocent those girls were in the mid-1960s.*

*Later that decade came many changes. With the renewal of Vatican II, nuns were now emerging into the modern world. But throughout this time, reflection gave the capacity to put things in perspective and the distance to accept what happened. I left the college and became the General Superior.*

*And then I read Dorothy Day, and her love for the poor changed my life.*

*It was the 1980s and the number of homeless was growing. I had spent decades at the college, beginning in the Registrar's Office and finishing as the Dean of Students. I had been in Congregational leadership for 11 years and then took a sabbatical for a year. When I returned, I did volunteer work in jails and with battered women. After seeing the terrible conditions in the shelters for women—the lack of privacy— I realized that I couldn't change that system.*

*However, I recognized the Incarnational—that all of those women were created in the image and likeness of God—and I continued to develop the capacity to work with women. There is enough psychic energy released by virtue of the Resurrection for all of us to do what we need to do.*

*I met with Sr. Yolanda and we started Visitation House, taking in women and their children, helping them get an education and career training. We lived in the house together with the women and shared our meals and our time with them. It isn't a short-term intervention. The women stay for more than a year and then move to the apartment building next door. It is a great ministry.*

*Now I spend my time working with Sr. Dot on Women's Global Connection. We are connected to groups of women around the world, and are working with women in Bukoba, Tanzania; Mongu, Zambia; and Chimbote, Peru. I am so encouraged when I see the growth among these women. It is life-giving.*

Throughout our conversation, it was clear to me that Sr. Neomi shared herself with every person she encountered. Seeing to their needs, caring for them—whether it was a small child struggling with spelling words, a young woman breaking up with a boyfriend, a mother with nowhere to stay, a Sister struggling to decide what her path should be—Sr. Neomi brought her kindness, strength and understanding to each situation. Joy to the world.

And now she brings her joy to me. Sparkling with that winsome, charming smile. Sharing memories of a life of caring for others. Talking with me about the headlines in *The New York Times*, her sharp analysis and critical wisdom advancing and challenging my own point of view. Helping me think through issues at the office. Providing a simple hospitality that is a balm for the soul.

Many times, when I am working at their home, I can see her through the double doors that lead to the patio and the garden. She is a gardener with her old straw hat and oversized gloves and cardigan sweater. She feeds the birds and waters the geraniums on the patio. The bougainvillea towers over her and she carefully snips each bush, bringing in the tissue paper hot pink and orange blossoms for the small shrine in the living room.

Joy to the world.

# The Journey to Emmaus: Living the Spirit

*Now that same day two of them were going to a village called Emmaus, about seven miles from Jerusalem. They were talking with each other about everything that had happened. Luke 24:13-14*

It was a crisp wet October day when the brown leaves were slick underfoot and the chill went to the bone. I had one last meeting before driving to El Puente, the Sisters' outreach ministry to the Latinx in Jefferson City, Missouri. The meeting was only to last for about an hour, giving me plenty of time to arrive before dinner. I was looking forward to spending a relaxing evening with Sr. Peggy Bonnot, CCVI, before visiting El Puente the next day.

Our Sisters had been in Jefferson City for decades. Several worked in the parish school, but two of them, Sr. Peggy and Sr. Margaret Snyder, CCVI, had founded

El Puente along with Sr. Marianne Kramer, CCVI, a Sister who had since moved on. Sr. Peggy is a quiet introvert. Calm and gentle, she has the gift of presence, and she is comfortable working directly with immigrants. The rural economy of Missouri depended upon these families from Mexico, Ecuador, Peru and Honduras, but there was little in the way of support. As a Jefferson City native, Sr. Peggy is hospitable and down to earth and continually welcomes these new families into the community.

El Puente literally means "bridge." I remembered how it had started as CCVI Mid-Missouri Ministry. It was that vague, just the seed of an idea to work directly with women and families who had come up from the Southern border looking for a better life. They had many needs. El Puente is there for them and continues to grow organically. The Sisters organize language classes, women's circles, and sacramental preparation. The immigrants need help with medical appointments, and the Sisters respond by serving as translators and providing transportation.

El Puente answers the Sisters' original call, "Our Lord Jesus Christ, suffering in the persons of a multitude of the sick and infirm of every kind, seeks relief at your hands."

These words had spawned a ministry of healing. And a ministry of celebration. The Sisters rejoiced in Baptisms and Quinceaneras. They organized processions for the Feast of Our Lady of Guadalupe each December followed by Las Posadas, the Christmas procession where children took the roles of the Holy Family searching for a place to stay in the same way that their families had come searching for a home in a sometimes hostile land.

I always enjoyed being with the Sisters at El Puente as they happily shared their families' stories. I was looking forward to this short break with them since I had been working with several colleagues on a difficult project to help youth in our community. Our collaboration had been fractious, and tempers were fraying, so much so that my co-worker, Mike Fitzgerald, had refused to work on the project at all. Decisions that some members of our group thought were final were changed unexpectedly. Several members took actions that others, including me, thought broke trust with the group. This meeting would hopefully clear the air.

One hour lapsed and we were still arguing over what to do. I was annoyed and frustrated because I knew it was past time for me to leave. As the minutes ticked by, I could see I was going to be very late. We were closing in on the second hour mark when I stepped out and called Sr. Peggy.

I told her I still hadn't left. She was dismayed and told me that she had invited the Sisters' lay Associates to have dinner with us. They were looking forward to meeting me. I felt guilty for letting her down and so I returned to the meeting and abruptly said I had to leave. Tempers were still running high and I caught several frowns as I quickly walked out the door.

The overcast skies had given over to a pounding rain as I drove onto the highway right before rush hour. As soon as I left the city behind and hit the open road, I stepped on the gas. The miles flew by past sodden harvested fields and sprinklings of billboards while I drove through the storm, turning the meeting over in my mind.

When had this project taken such a dark turn? Was it more about egos, being in charge, getting our way, taking credit? What happened to our focus on the young people who had so many needs? When had we lost the respect and collegiality that had been a hallmark of our work in the past? What had changed?

I reflected on the story of the disciples walking to Emmaus, encountering Christ, and then inviting Him to dinner. My colleagues and I had started on the journey together, but over the past year we had strayed from the path as our motivations and perspectives grew further apart.

I thought about why the Foundation was doing this. Obviously, providing opportunities for young people was in keeping with the Incarnate Word Foundation mission. But somehow along the way, that sense of mission had not stayed with me. I ran through all the things I would have liked to have said in the meeting. Harsh words. Sarcastic and cutting comments. The angrier I became, the more I accelerated into the thunderstorm. Soon I was hitting 80 as the lightning ripped the dusky sky and a trip that should have taken 2 hours was completed in record time. I was not even late for dinner.

During our meal, the women and Sr. Peggy talked about the work they were doing at El Puente. First and foremost, it was a ministry of presence. Initially I was distracted, still thinking back to the meeting that afternoon. But then Sr. Peggy talked about accompanying a woman in labor to the hospital and of staying there the entire time, for more than 24 hours. I could not imagine what it would be like to be in labor in a strange country, not knowing the language, in a hi-tech hospital with all sorts of caregivers in and out of the room, changing shifts. Sr. Peggy was a constant peaceful presence, translating the young woman's questions for the medical team, and sometimes just holding the young mother's hand.

Later that night, Sr. Peggy and I sat in comfortable easy chairs with a cup of tea in the Mid-century, split-level ranch she and the Sisters called home. In her soft Midwestern voice, she talked about her family and growing up in Jefferson City, and I could see the roots of her practical approach to life. Everything about Sr. Peggy, from her soft cardigan sweater to her quiet voice and calm eyes spoke to me of an inner tranquility rooted in encountering God in the ordinary events of everyday life. She found fulfillment in walking with immigrants and sorting through the recurring challenges they faced in building a life for their families in a foreign community.

We watched her cat, Blue, meander around the room as I told her about why I was late. She listened intently as I ran through the entire history of the youth project, the recriminations and the fraying relationships clear to see. Sr. Peggy made no comment but just listened. Her patient presence calmed me down and I finally relaxed.

The conversation turned to what was going on at El Puente. The Sisters had decided to open a satellite site in California and Sr. Margaret Snyder, a quilter, had moved there. I was stunned. How could they expand to California? Sr. Peggy chuckled and reiterated, "California, Missouri." A large Hispanic community was forming in that small town because of the abundant employment at local factories. The evening wound down and we called it a night.

The next morning, I visited with the staff at El Puente. As I was leaving, Sr. Peggy came outside and called me back. "I have thought about what you told me last night," she said quietly, "and I think you should quit working on the youth project. The Spirit is not present. They may well accomplish their goals, but it will never be everything it could have been because the mission is not front and center. Because of that, it is better to let it go rather than continue on and have the relationships be destroyed." She gave me a gentle hug and waved to me as I drove away.

That day I learned there are many journeys to Emmaus. On that one evening, Sr. Peggy had walked with me.

# Packing the Trunk:
# Answering the Call

The Feast of the Assumption is a special feast day for our Sisters, a date which commemorates Mary's ascension into heaven. In years past, it was the day when our Sisters would pack their trunks and open the letter that would indicate where they would serve in the upcoming year.

When the feast day dawned, the Sisters in San Antonio would gather in the Chapel. Each Sister had an assigned stall in the order in which she had entered. The hand-carved oaken stalls faced the middle aisle, allowing the Sisters to pray together, with each side of the chapel taking a part and praying back and forth, a legacy of their monastic founding. The Chapel walls are illuminated by scenes from the life of Christ enshrined in stained glass. The altar frames a relief of the Annunciation, where another woman answered a call that would set in motion the Incarnation that would lead to hundreds of women sitting in this Chapel to answer the continuing call.

Every August 15th, each Sister would receive a brief letter that began, "The Incarnate Word asks you. . ." and then the assignment would follow. The Sisters would leave immediately for those assignments. Often, they would be sent to a new city with no idea of what they would be doing once they arrived at the convent. They could be teaching first grade or seventh. The need determined the work. I wondered how they opened the letter. Were some Sisters tentative or did others just rip it open? Did the more fastidious Sisters bring a small sewing scissors in one of their habit pockets and slit the envelope?

Answering a call in that way, going where you are sent, is totally foreign to me. To set aside your own preferences, your autonomy, and place yourself totally at the disposal of a mission in such an intentional way, and knowing that these seemingly arbitrary decisions will occur each year for the rest of your life, is almost unfathomable. Leaving behind friends and family, perhaps not even being able to say goodbye, not to mention packing everything I own in one black trunk...I don't know that I could do it. But the Sisters did for decades.

For some Sisters even their original assignment was not of their choosing. As Sr. Kathleen Coughlin, CCVI, told me:

*When I entered, I wanted to teach first grade because I love little kids and I knew I would never have any. However, that was at a time when they needed nurses. The Sisters said to me, 'You will be a nurse.' Well I almost died. The last thing I wanted to do was be a nurse. And that was one of the first wonderful lessons of life—let go and let God. I fought it but I finally decided, 'Well, hang around. If you leave in 3 years at least you will leave with an education.' In those days, our Sisters in education only did their degree work in summertime, and it took a lot longer for teaching Sisters to complete their degrees than for the nurses. So, let go and let God. In all of my ministry work, I have done that, and I have been nothing but blessed and enriched.*

A native St. Louisan, Sr. Kathleen's nursing career led her to become the CEO of one of the Sisters' largest hospitals, CHRISTUS Spohn Hospital in Corpus Christi. Her most recent turn in the road took her to the University of the Incarnate Word where she persuades donors to support the mission of a growing university with a new medical school. Her twinkly-eyed charm and eagle-eyed focus on getting people on board with the mission is something that is always present. I know she would have brought both to the classroom along with her sense of fun, but God had other plans.

Today our Sisters no longer receive a letter in a pew. They are partners in discerning their path. There are still times, however, when they are called upon to accept assignments and work in ministries that might not be their choice. Sr. Tere Maya, CCVI, reflected upon why Sisters accept this call:

> *In life, you set yourself a goal. You imagine your future. In my case it was, 'I'll be teaching one place and hopefully, I'll write a book.' That was my big thing. After I entered the Congregation, it was no longer my plans. It is our plans. It is a collective dreaming that we do together.*
>
> *The defining moments for me have been when I was asked to do something I could not even imagine doing. Things I had never even entertained as a possibility. Or living in a place I have had to go look up on a map. Those have been defining moments because they have allowed me to understand that it is not about what you do, or where you are doing it, or the job description you have. It is simply about being part of this bigger thing.*

# The String and the Kite:
## What is God Telling You?

Sr. Mary Margaret Bright, CCVI, always tells me that she is the string, and I am the kite. For several years, I was blessed with her presence in the office. I always referred to her as the resident wise woman. Her striking white hair and clear blue eyes are emphasized by the bright colors she always wears—striking teals and scarlets. I can't count the times I'd walk into her office with a new idea and she'd listen patiently and then laugh and say, "Oh, Bridget. I don't know how you come up with these ideas, but once you figure out what we are going to do about it then I'm happy to work on carrying it out. I am the string and you are the kite."

She is prose and I am poetry. I am intuitive. She's logical and has her doctorate in computer science which came in handy for me since every time I created a spreadsheet it never seemed to calculate correctly—a mystery she was frequently called upon to solve. Put our differences together and we complete one another. Together we are the string and the kite. The kite needs the string to keep it from soaring too high into the stratosphere, and the string needs the kite to stretch. A perfect match.

One piece of wisdom she imparted to me was how to look for a sign. In hindsight that seems odd, because Sr. Mary Margaret is typically firmly rooted in reality, a legacy of her German-American roots. But when I would come to her when I seemingly had hit a dead end in a project, or when I was aggravated with something–or someone–after listening patiently, there were times when she'd give me advice or would help solve the problem. Other times, however, she would give me a serious look and say, "What is God telling you?"

My immediate thought was, "What do you mean, what is God telling me? This situation is urgent. It's frustrating. Most importantly, I want to know what to do now."

Sometimes, however, the answer doesn't come immediately, and even if the answer does appear in a flash of intuition, that answer may not be the right one. There are times when setting a problem aside, taking time to be more objective and not acting in the heat of the moment, is the better approach. Asking what God is telling me means examining my own part in whatever the issue or problem is. What is my part in this situation? Is there a role for me to be part of the solution? And even harder, what have I done that might have caused this, or even made things worse?

"What is God telling you?" is a challenge.

When she retired to San Antonio, the question wasn't what God was telling me, but what was God telling Sr. Mary Margaret. The message was clear: It was time to go to the bus station. It was time to work with the immigrants and refugees coming to San Antonio from the border:

> *When women and children are released from the immigration detention centers, either the family has to pay a bond or they put ankle bracelets on them, and then their family in the United States sends either a bus or airplane ticket and they are dropped off in San Antonio. Many of them end up at the bus terminal.*
>
> *A Presbyterian minister trained in St. Louis started a group called Interfaith Welcome Coalition. It is definitely interfaith—not only Presbyterians, but Lutherans, Catholics and people from other faith traditions. One group from the churches prepares a backpack with snacks, toothbrushes, a small throw blanket because the buses are very cold, water, and coloring books and crayons for the children. The most the families ever have with them are two cloth grocery bags with their possessions, with rare exceptions.*
>
> *I give them the backpack and a lunch made by Loaves and Fishes. I enjoy being with the children, giving the girls dolls and the boys toy cars. We help*

*the families with their tickets. We have a map of the United States and we explain to them where they are going and where they will need to change buses. And they are totally lost. You can tell that some of the women are more educated, and others are from small villages where they speak their native language, not Spanish. There have also been a few families from Africa and Brazil, and occasionally we have a Romanian family. We give them a small piece of paper they can show people when they need to change buses to help them find the right bus. I don't speak Spanish, but I still am able to help in this small way.*

*What happens next for them? They may be going to the East or West coast. Some have gone as far as Boston. And eventually they will go before the immigration court to see if they receive refugee status. The court system is so backed up it will take two or three years before they have a hearing. If a woman goes unaccompanied to the court the chances that she will receive asylum are extremely low, especially given that she may not even speak English. There are immigration lawyers who are doing pro bono work, but there are not nearly enough of them.*

*The next time you are in the airport, there may come a time when you see a woman with children carrying two green grocery bags. If you do, don't walk by, but stop and see if they need help finding the next plane. Imagine what it must be for these women who have never been to a busy airport, or even been on an airplane, trying to find their gate. Can you imagine? It is my privilege to help these families.*

Sometimes the string keeps a kite from flying too high. Other times, a string is truly a lifeline.

# Bougainvillea: Finding the Garden

The drive from the airport in Mexico City begins with triple-decker freeways, then turns to crowded boulevards and finally gives way to the neighborhood of San Ángel. Flower shops throw rainbows of blossoms on the sidewalk down the hilly street from upscale shops and homes. The journey ends on a steep, narrow, uneven cobblestone lane bordered by garden walls, concrete facades, and garage doors that come right to the edge of the small sidewalks. Casa San Ángel has a similar design. The garage door and entrance border the street, and vivid fuchsia bougainvillea spill over the top of the high wall.

The complex is large, with a quiet convent, administrative offices, meeting rooms, visitor parlors, a garage, a large chapel, and a retirement community. The buildings are connected by a labyrinth of windowed corridors. Whenever I stay there, I never fail to get lost.

After being buzzed through the doors, steep steps take you to the doorway and you find yourself in a wood-paneled reception area with a glistening terrazzo floor and gentle light filtering through frosted glass. The waiting room beyond the doors is dimly lit and so quiet it's as if someone had just tiptoed through whispering, "Shhh." A vase of roses sits beneath a dark portrait of Christ as a young boy, the iconic image of the Incarnate Word, and an elaborate painting in the Spanish colonial style of a crowned Mary holding her Son hangs over a wooden antique settee and side chairs.

Nestled among the buildings, and visible through the corridor windows, is a beautifully manicured garden. Everywhere you turn there are immaculate grey-tiled pathways bordered with vivid periwinkle blue agapanthus, bright splotches of snapdragons, regal orange bird-of-paradise, and plush hydrangeas. The faint pink walls of the buildings fade into the background as you listen to the birds and stroll past shade trees, conifers, and small fruit and fig trees scattered throughout the manicured lawns.

I stop by a large shrine where a beautiful statue of Our Lady of Guadalupe is surrounded by a small, turquoise-tiled pool. The statue is shaded by a pointed concrete arbor with an interior scattered with the stars of the night sky. The fuchsia bougainvillea I had spied from the street clambers up buildings and walls, joined by hot pink and white–bearing vines. When I had entered the convent gate that morning, I had no idea that this beautiful garden is what I would find inside, a perfect place for prayer and reflection.

Getting to know the Mexican Sisters is an invitation to another private garden. When I first came to Mexico, I was impressed by their serious attention to the mission and their warm hospitality. At the international meetings, I noticed that those of us from the States were quick to advance our ideas, ticking through the steps with Power-Point precision. The Mexican Sisters wove their thought process through an analysis of what the reality of the situation was, coupled with theological reflection.

On the one hand, I found them to be more formal than the Sisters I knew in the States. On the other, Sr. Maria de Jesús Bringas Aguirre, CCVI, was quick to drop everything to take time with me at the Basilica of Our Lady of Guadalupe or go to Xochimilco, the Floating Gardens.

When I arrived in Mexico City only to find a meeting had been cancelled, Sr. Tere Maya spent the day giving me a private tour of the Musco Nacional de Antropologia, carefully explaining the history of the peoples of pre-Columbian Mexico, the Olmecs, Aztecs, and other nations.

Another evening, several of us drove through the central plaza on Mexican Independence Day to see the huge red, white, and green light displays on the sides of the government buildings. We ended up at Mariachi Plaza, where strolling groups of musicians serenaded the crowd. It was quite an education and after days of work, we relaxed together and had a good time.

My inability to speak Spanish was no longer a barrier. Over time, I came to know Sisters as individuals, with different life experiences, interests and points of view, and ultimately as good friends whom I love.

Relationships are not instantaneous, especially when you have to take time to learn another person's culture. Like the flowers in the garden, deep friendships require nurturing and time to come to fruition. The courtyard garden at Casa San Ángel is the product of years of care, and a beautiful garden to enjoy.

One of my good friends is Sr. Maria Luisa Vélez Garcia, CCVI.

I first met Sr. Maria Luisa when we were both staying at the Generalate in San Antonio. The rooms there are small, and I went down to the community room where I found her sorting through some sewing notions and thread. She told me about the daycare center she had established in a low-income area of Mexico City. The people in the Santa Fe area had embraced the center, and when I visited it some years later, it was a neighborhood anchor.

Sr. Maria Luisa has worked in schools, out in the community among those in need, and in development. She has short, simply styled grey hair, a ready smile and kind brown eyes. Her love of the mission also propelled her into congregational leadership at a time when the Sisters were working through new directions after Vatican II. One day over lunch at Casa San Ángel, she shared her journey with me:

*I come from a large family of ten—four brothers and five sisters. The school bus went to my parents' house for 33 years. I always wanted to work with the poor, and when I finished my studies, I went to work at a school our Sisters had in Mexico City, Claudio Maria Dubuis, that served low-income families. I became a lay principal at age 18.*

*I had always planned to get married and when I decided to enter the convent, my family was very upset. They didn't want me to enter the Congregation-- my father, mother, brothers, sisters, no one. My father said, 'You don't belong to them,' but I knew it was right for me because when I asked the Sisters, 'Do you work with the poor?' they answered, 'Yes, we work with the poor.' That was it for me.*

*I was part of the last group in Mexico to wear the formal habit and then we shifted to a modified habit. Times were changing and I wanted to work directly with the poor rather than in one of our schools. However, the Sister who was the Provincial said, 'You must go where you are sent,' and so I went to the school in Tampico, Mexico. Tampico is on a bay with hot humid weather, and within a few months we experienced a hurricane and ended up having to build a new school.*

*At that time, the Province would move the newer Sisters to see if we truly had a vocation, and so in the middle of the school year I was sent to Miguel Ángel, but only for a year. After that, I went to Chihuahua to teach. I thought, 'God, why are they moving me around so much? Perhaps I am not good at my job.' I could not say anything, because we were not allowed at that time to question decisions. At the end of the school year the Sisters told me I was being sent to study formation, and that is when I finally spoke up. I really wanted to be a teacher, and they agreed.*

*I studied for my master's degree in the summers after teaching during the school year, and in seven years, I received my Master's Degree in Education. That is when they asked me to become the principal of Miguel Ángel. We had 2,400 students. I was happy there, and then I was elected to the Provincial leadership team where I was responsible for all of our schools.*

Sr. Maria Luisa's time in leadership corresponded with a time of transition that involved difficult choices:

*When I came to leadership, we began to see a change as some of our Sisters spoke up and said they wanted to work in Pastoral Popular, that is working with the poor in the community. We went back and studied our founders, Bishop Dubuis and the early Sisters. A group of us, about 40 Sisters, delved into our history and spirituality. We looked deep into our charism and began writing and talking about what it really meant.*

*After that we had our first Assembly as a Congregation. Vatican II was definitely affecting us. Many Sisters left the Congregation. They felt we were not moving quickly enough to do what Vatican II directed. Others left because they felt the Congregation was not the same as the one that they had entered. They said they could not support the new direction, and they preferred to leave. It happened in Mexico, in San Antonio, and in St. Louis.*

*That is when I began to study liberation theology. Everyone in my classes was coming from that perspective, and there were so many new ideas about a theology of liberation and revelation. It wasn't easy to bring these ideas to the Congregation because back then we were very conservative.*

*After my three years in provincial leadership, at the Chapter meeting of the entire Congregation, Sr. Neomi Hayes said to me, 'Luisa, you better be prepared because you may be elected to the General Council for the entire Congregation.' Back then, the elections were quite secret, and I suddenly found myself at the Generalate. I was only 38 years old.*

*Sr. Neomi and Sr. Dot Ettling were on the team too and I was close to them. This was the 19th Chapter, and things were changing. Before, there had been one Sister from Mexico on the General Council, but she was responsible only for matters related to Mexico. If the Council was discussing an issue about the St. Louis or San Antonio province, the Mexican Sister was not included in the meeting. She was purposely left out, even though the full Council would weigh in on issues that concerned Mexico.*

*When I was elected, I told them, 'If my role is going to be like the Mexican Councilor's role in the past, I do not accept. I want to be a full member of the Generalate.' That was a new concept, and they agreed.*

*Living in San Antonio was difficult. At that time, I didn't know much English. I did not want to rely on a translator. The Sisters already had their own lives there, and I was lonely. Weekends were hard. I remember one Sister who would see me and say, 'Hello, Chiquita,' and I said, 'Sister, I am not Chiquita. I have a name. My name is Maria Luisa. And the Sisters from Mexico are not Chiquitas. Each one of us has a name.' I dealt with things like that many times, and I would say to Sr. Dot, 'this is not just.' Sr. Dot agreed, 'This is not only not just, but we should talk about it. Let's talk.'*

*The first year was hard. The second was better, and then by the third year I was happy. Sr. Neomi and Sr. Dot really helped me. Our friendship deepened. They gave me the freedom to be the person I wanted to be in the Congregation. The ministry of Pastoral Popular began to grow in Mexico. I began working with the Sisters to form Las Hermanas for the Hispanic sisters, priests and brothers. We encouraged them to recognize and bring their own culture to their ministry–to be proud of their culture.*

*I helped form our lay missionary program. We began with two from Ireland, two from the States, and one from Mexico. All of them worked with the poor.*

After her time in leadership, Sr. Maria Luisa was able to do the work she loved, caring for the poor.

*After I finished, I worked through the Vatican and was able to work in many countries in Latin America as part of Pastoral Popular. I went to places in Brazil, Bolivia, Chile, Peru, and Colombia. When I came back, I was asked to go to work with the poor in Mexico City by the bishop. I stayed there for 14 years. We worked together with the people.*

*I noticed that mothers did not have anyone to watch their children while they were working. Leaving the children at home alone was dangerous, and I asked the people, 'I see this need, but what do you think?' We gave a questionnaire to more than 1,500 people and they agreed. We started a center for 50 children, but one day the opportunity came to acquire a larger building that was perfect for our needs. A woman's godmother was selling her home. I still don't know exactly how we found the money. We bought the house, restored it, and it is where we have the child center now.*

*For me, it all comes back to serving the poor. In the Santa Fe community, I worked with very poor people—people addicted to drugs, to alcohol, and young girls who were already mothers. It is very hard for them, and people expect them to get off the streets and change. I said, 'Where do you want them to go? They cannot pay for a place to stay. They have nothing.'*

*We need to reach out to the poor. We need to be inclusive—involving them in decisions, bringing the resources they need and to walking with them. We, as Sisters, needed to go back to our roots. And that is what the Mexican Sisters have brought to the Congregation through Pastoral Popular. The preferential option for the poor, the emphasis on peace and justice, are a call from Vatican II, but those are also deep in our roots.*

# Chiapas: How Are You in Your Heart

Several years ago, I traveled to Chiapas, Mexico with the Sisters for an immersion trip to visit their ministry, Nich Klum Café. We touched down in Villahermosa in inky darkness and traveled to the heart of the city, where bars down the street from our small motel were doing a brisk and noisy business. The next morning, we traveled by bus up to the clear air of the mountains in Chiapas.

It was my first trip to the Yucatan. The verdant slumbering hills held Mayan ruins and our home base was a coffee plantation owned by the Ch'ol Indians. The Sisters have been partners in Nich Klum Café for decades, working with the tribe to build an international coffee company. During that week I learned the mechanics of growing organic coffee—from seedlings sprouting in the greenhouse to beans ripening in the fields. Working together, the Sisters and the workers had created a cooperative to market the coffee which was grown on the fertile tribal lands in the mountains. The best coffee was shipped to Europe, the second-best to the United States and the rest was left for Mexico.

Our Sisters worked hand in glove with the people, a true ministry of what they called *Pastoral Popular*, serving the myriad needs of the people and being a presence integrated into the community. Nich Klum Café headquarters and the convent shared the same buildings. The Sisters were trusted business advisors and dear friends of the men who worked at the coffee cooperative.

Gregorio was my guide. He was in his mid-40s, with the stocky build and dark skin of the Ch'ol tribe. He spoke four languages—I speak one. We met each day, beginning with breakfast. He gave me tours of the coffee greenhouse and explained the careful ways they nurtured the coffee plants on the mountain terraces and developed protocols to ensure that the coffee growing techniques were organic.

Meals were served in a small room in a cement block and stucco building that dated from the 1950s, and the opaque louvered windows opened onto a courtyard of tropical foliage and flowers. Breakfast consisted of bowls of black beans, fresh fruit, cellophane-wrapped Bimbo cakes, and hot coffee.

On the first morning I was presented with a whole mango. As I clumsily attempted to slice it in the bowl, Gregorio had a harder and harder time keeping a straight face. Finally, he and several of the Sisters burst out laughing. They picked up their mangoes, stuck them on forks to create what resembled a mango popsicle and proceeded to elegantly peel and slice them. I laughed too, and followed suit with a little less flair.

The conversation shifted to what had been our worse meals ever. Mine was some sausages of indeterminate origin in Cologne. Gregorio's was at a McDonald's in Barcelona. I was humbled to realize that not only did he speak four languages, but he was also Nich Klum's marketing director, frequently traveling to Europe, their most lucrative market. I learned we both had daughters. His were at university. Mine were younger. His wife was from the Tikal tribe. My spouse was Irish-American.

He told me about his village high in the mountains that he visited each weekend, and how he had rebuilt his home three times, first of sticks, then of mud bricks, and now of cement blocks. I thought of my cozy arts and crafts bungalow a stone's throw from the bluffs of the Mississippi. But despite the completely different circumstances surrounding our lives, at the essence we had much in common. We were proud of our daughters and had dreams for their futures. We could laugh over mangoes. And neither of us liked McDonald's.

At the start of each day, his greeting translated not as, "How are you?" but as "How are you in your heart?"

I was struck by the contrast of the typical greeting in the States, where people asked, "How are you?" The expected answer is "Fine," or at the very least, "Okay." It is a superficial question. A conversation that ends with, "Have a nice day."

The Sisters in Chiapas are women with wonderful administrative abilities. At various times in their lives, they had served in Congregational leadership in Mexico City or taught in the Sisters' schools throughout Mexico. They had chosen to leave behind the amenities of those assignments and live simply among the people of Chiapas. They had chosen a place where the question asked each day is "How are you in your heart?", a question that places us in relationship.

As I was learning from our Sisters, relationship is not just where we find common bonds, but in their worldview, it is where God dwells. Several Incarnate Word Sisters find that with the people in Chiapas, and while I was with them at Nich Klum Café, I found God in those ordinary conversations with my guide, Gregorio, as well.

# Table Sharing:
# Creating Communities of Love

Prior to Vatican II, our Sisters lived in convents, some of which could accommodate more than 100 Sisters. Over the past few decades that has changed for a variety of reasons. Living in smaller groups creates more of a sense of community. Sometimes it was more convenient to live closer to work. Parishes wanted to repurpose convents to meet other needs, like adding a preschool, a learning center, or more classrooms. The vision of Sr. Cathy Vetter, CCVI, was living in a neighborhood and being with the people.

Sr. Cathy was one of the first Sisters I met when I came to the Foundation. Sr. Cathy brings a creative spirit and a vibrant enthusiasm to her work. She is vivacious with salt and pepper short hair and an enthusiastic smile. She loves people, the color purple, snowflakes, the Osage River, and grows fabulous tomatoes.

She felt strongly that the Sisters should establish a presence in South St. Louis. She found her first neighborhood house in St. Pius X Parish on South Grand, on the fringe of a neighborhood of ethnic restaurants and small shops. It is a neighborhood in transition, and one that welcomes immigrants. Sr. Cathy shared her thoughts on the importance of sharing a table with neighbors:

*I am not bilingual, but I lead with my heart and I love people, and that is what God calls us to do. I hear Pope Francis saying, 'What you need to be about as women religious is people of joy, people of love.' When Sr. Mary Henry, Sr. Jean Durel and I found the house on McKean, we consciously wanted to be among the immigrants. We wanted to try to be a stable and welcoming presence in a neighborhood.*

*Sr. Feliciana Mejia told me years ago that if you envision something, it will happen. When we moved into this neighborhood, my vision was that the day would come when I will bake bread, the neighbors will smell it and come to the door. We will sit on the porch and they will eat warm bread. That was my vision. And that is what happened. I baked bread. The neighbors just to the east are Ethiopians. They have a little boy, Samuel, the twins, and a baby girl. The twins were waiting outside that morning and their mom was holding the baby. I came out and I had two strawberries in my hand.*

*Just as I walked out of the door, the boys started calling, 'Cathy! Cathy!' and then I went down the stairs and we hugged each other. We talked to each other. They were my neighbors, and they were my friends. That is what it is about, talking to others and having a relationship. Even though I was working out in the suburbs at a large parish, my life is different because when I come home, I come home to diversity.*

*The family who lived on the other side of our house were from Afghanistan. I met the mother, and even though we did not have much language, it was my heart going out to them. I would smile and wave, and the children would smile, wave back, and say, 'Hi.' I loved these people, and I would sit in the house and think of their faces, and pray for them. We built a community.*

*That community kept growing. Two young couples bought houses across the street. They cut my grass and took care of it. Our backyard became the community garden. One morning I was talking to my Ethiopian neighbor and she said, 'They are cleaning your village. They are taking care of your village.' I said, 'Yes, they are. We are all part of the village and they are helping. They're taking care of our village.' It's a wonderful image, and when she said that, she said, 'They are taking care of your village,' and that she didn't say, 'your yard,' because on that block we became a little village.*

*One evening, three young people from across the street had supper together with us because I had a big pot of soup. They kept saying, 'Well, we are a community now,' and I said, 'Yes, we are a community,' and we are. This is what needs to happen for our world to be a smaller place. Of those four people, I know that at least three of them have spent time in other countries already, working and volunteering, and that is what they are about. They are about the bigger picture, and they are about the community.*

*That is why I came to religious life, for community. It doesn't matter what I am doing—it's about community. My God relationship is nurtured in this community here with young people, the refugees, the immigrants, and the multi-cultural richness of St. Pius X parish. God is the love between us. If two or three gather, it is the God-ness that makes the community among us. People hunger for that in their heart. That is the hunger. You can't always name it.*

*When we can sit around in this room and talk about these things, then I look forward to having more community meals with them and gardening with them and having those conversations. 'What does that mean for you? What is the hunger that calls you to community?' It is the interrelatedness, not only of our earth but also of our cosmos, all of that.*

For Sister Cathy, the Incarnation and her ministry of presence to people in the community is about love:

*My aunt, Sister Carina, was a Sister of Loretto. At the end of her life, when she was 94 years old, I'd call her and she'd say, 'It's love, love, love. I love you. I want you to know I love you. It is all about love. Everything is about love.' During the last days of her life, that's what she knew. I want to learn it before the last days of my life, because I really believe that is it. Relationships and relational skills are hard to learn sometimes. That's what we need to focus on. That is what Jesus did and that is what Pope Francis is doing.*

*We have to change the way we do things. We have to create small communities of love and of table sharing. That's what Jesus did—table sharing. We call it Eucharist now, and that's what we need to do with our friends, and with our neighbors who become our new friends. That will feed us. When we are fed that way, then we have something to give. If I am not fed that way, then I don't have something to give. It is so important, and people hunger for it.*

Now Sr. Cathy is building another small community at the Novitiate House, not far from the house on McKean. She and a new community of Sisters are building raised beds for another community garden. They are reaching out to new neighbors and welcoming old friends to share the table and build another community of love.

# Going to Gruene:
# Finding Fulfillment in Relationships

Sr. Cindy Stacy, CCVI, is a Texan whose wisdom comes from the dry beauty of the Hill Country where blue bonnets startle the eye for a brief season. It is a world of solid limestone buildings built by German immigrants, of pecan trees, lizards, and brush. When I first met Sr. Cindy, I was struck by the quiet that surrounds her. She is deliberate in her approach. She thinks before she says it, but when she says it, she means it.

A social worker by training, she spent her days at Visitation House helping young women and their children transition from homelessness to self-sufficiency. When the families first came, they lived with Sr. Cindy, Sr. Yolanda Tarango, CCVI, and Sr. Leticia de Jesús Rodriguez Hernández, CCVI, in the Sisters' home, a large white house with a wide two-story veranda supported by huge round pillars.

What had once been an airy home for the elite of San Antonio now housed women and children who were making an independent life for themselves with the Sisters' help. The Sisters literally opened their home to these families, living right down the hall from them. The formal parlor had been converted to a large playroom, while another room on the main floor was used for tutoring. In the evening, everyone shared a meal in the spacious dining room. Donated knickknacks created a homey atmosphere.

Whenever I went to San Antonio, I tried to connect with the Sisters at Visitation House. Usually we would meet for dinner at a modest restaurant—once, Sr. Yolanda and I managed to eat for under ten dollars at a pancake place, and we always joked about that. Other times, if a new family was in the house, we'd just order pizza, sit at the large Victorian dining room table, and relax afterwards in their community room.

Sr. Cindy is a fisherwoman and that suits her. It demands silence, concentration, and patience, none of which is a virtue of mine. One hot afternoon, Sr. Cindy and I went to the Guadalupe River. While she fished, I dangled in the water, barefoot, knitting. She caught a few sunfish and before she released them, I admired each one. It was a beautiful afternoon. We didn't talk much but relaxed in the easy comfort of being in the close proximity of a friend.

That evening we went to Gruene, a Texas Hill Country town. The old mill town had evolved into a gathering spot for musicians with outdoor pavilions and restaurants vying for the tourist trade. A restaurant in the old mill itself overlooked the Guadalupe River and we sat on a balcony high above the murmuring water with a slight chill in the air.

My husband and I were adjusting to an empty nest. Both of our girls were grown and would probably not return home. No more book bags by the door or pounding footsteps rushing down the worn oak steps in the morning. An emptiness was settling in.

My response to this was to engage in a flurry of activities. A new book club. A new committee at my parish. A new Board appointment. More mugs and pots at the studio for shelves already filled. I was certainly busy, but not busy enough to not miss the girls terribly.

As I described the many ways I was planning to fill my time, Sr. Cindy looked increasingly bemused. A small smile flickered, and her soft grey eyes crinkled as she slightly shook her head.

Then Sr. Cindy explained why what I was doing was not working. All of the ways I was finding to spend my time were off target. While at first glance the activities of daily life had changed when the girls left, in reality the deeper change was relational. More activities did not address that fundamental shift. That, Sr. Cindy said, was the essence of the issue.

Her prescription focused exclusively on the need for relationship. Finding ways to occupy the time isn't the answer. If anything, the intensifying of activity only emphasized the dissatisfaction and the void. It is also the easy path, because deepening relationships is challenging and demands staying in touch with both your inner self and theirs. The real need isn't superficial; it is deep, and the answer is to deepen the time spent.

In her quiet way, Sr. Cindy outlined another pathway that involved spending more time with the people who really matter, family members and close friends. The answer is deepening those relationships. Her wisdom is living the Sisters' spirituality, that God is among us and present in our relationships with others. Whenever I am tempted to take on yet another activity, I think back to that quiet afternoon on the Guadalupe River with a quiet fisherwoman admiring the translucent beauty of a sunfish dangling from a hook until she releases it into the current, and I, too, am swept away by the love a deep friendship brings.

# Amazing Grace: The Journey Begins with a Blessing

In response to the millennium, the Sisters decided to begin a new mission. They spent quite some time discerning where to go, and finally it was down to two possibilities: Haiti or Zambia. Both countries are among the world's most economically impoverished. Bishop Claude Dubuis had written in 1866 to Rev. Mother Angelique Hiver to prepare Sisters to respond to the cholera epidemics in Texas. At the millennium, Bishop Paul Duffy, an Oblate of Mary Immaculate from San Antonio serving in Zambia, invited the Sisters to Mongu to work in his new diocese with women and children suffering from HIV/AIDS. After months of discernment, the Sisters determined that they must go and serve the families in need of their care.

The Sisters began a relationship with German Holy Cross Sisters who had served in Mongu for decades and were to stay with them in their compound on the outskirts of Mongu.

After a few years, I received an invitation as well. Women's Global Connection (WGC), our Sisters' women's empowerment ministry, was sending a group to Mongu and they invited me to come along to teach micro-lending. I had never been to Africa and I was quite excited to go. I also didn't know much about micro-lending other than what I had read in Mohammad Unis' book about the Grameen Bank, but I gamely prepared a PowerPoint and printed handouts. My goal was to establish a micro-lending group with women from the Lozi tribe.

Our contingent was small, three women from San Antonio and me. Sr. Dot Ettling was our leader. I had stayed with her and Sr. Neomi many times in San Antonio, and her enthusiasm was infectious. Sr. Dot was in her early 70s and one of the Congregation's visionaries. While she taught full-time at the University of the Incarnate Word in the doctoral program, she also led WGC. Her enthusiasm was remarkable. When I was with Sr. Dot, I believed I could do anything.

As the time for our departure grew near, I began to have a few doubts. I went for my vaccinations and my spouse began mumbling about mysterious diseases transmitted by monkey bites. I started collecting vacuum-packed tuna packets and individually wrapped cheese and Ritz cracker snacks in case the food was problematic. I worried that the trip would be depressing and struggled with the idea that I would be a poverty tourist. I realized I didn't know the first thing about micro-lending, really. Finally I concluded that the best possible scenario would be to plan the trip, not go on it, and then pretend it had happened and that it was a transformational experience that I had thoroughly enjoyed.

I went to San Antonio shortly before the Zambia trip would occur. I was walking through the atrium of the Sisters' retirement community and there she was, Sr. Grace O'Meara, CCVI, a winsome little woman with an iron will and an Irish brogue. She was charming and opinionated at the same time. With Sr. Grace, I could see that you could easily end up agreeing to all sorts of things and then wonder afterward how that had ever even happened.

Sr. Grace had spent decades in Peru as a missionary and then moved on to Zambia. Being a missionary was in her bones and even though she was in San Antonio recuperating from an illness and could easily retire, she was counting the days until she could return.

I told her I was going to Mongu in a few weeks, and she was overjoyed. She told me about the work she was doing at a preschool, and how wonderful the children were. Families in Mongu made great sacrifices to send their children to school, and one obstacle was a lack of school uniform shorts. I thought of all the Catholic schoolchildren in St. Louis and the plethora of uniform shorts in every closet, and Sr. Grace quickly seized upon the idea that I could use my two suitcases to bring 100 pounds of uniform shorts to Mongu. It was an eight-hour drive from Lusaka and no courier or delivery service would bring goods there. A world without FedEx—I never really thought that there were places on earth where sending a package was impossible. Collecting the shorts would be easy. I could put the word out to the Catholic schools in St. Louis.

I knew that Sr. Dot would not be in favor of this. She was a firm believer that giving things away to the women in Zambia would create a skewed power dynamic and was patronizing. She had warned all of the trip participants not to bring things to give away.

In talking with Sr. Grace, I started to see things differently. The shorts wouldn't be coming from me. Sr. Grace would distribute the shorts as part of her work at the school. The shorts wouldn't be cast-offs but would be issued as school supplies. And as a mother myself, I knew that if my daughters didn't have uniforms to attend school, I wouldn't care where the uniforms were made or how they came to us, I would just want my daughters to have what they needed. Sr. Grace and I finalized our plan. Even though the sisters were worried about Sr. Grace's health, she was determined to return to Mongu and she would distribute the shorts as needed to the families at her school and others in Mongu.

St. Teresa of Avila said, "The feeling remains that God is on the journey, too." When we ended our spontaneous meeting, Sr. Grace put her hands on me and blessed me for the Zambian journey. I knew that I wouldn't be alone as I traveled to Mongu. Sr. Grace made sure of that. She gave me more than a spiritual blessing at her hands. She also gave me the gift of being able to help in a very small way. She gave me the gift of her joy in serving others, a joy that skipped over hardship and fear, and landed right with the people who gave love and joy in return.

She gave me amazing grace.

# Dancing the Circle:
# The Women of Mongu

On the 18-hour journey to Zambia, I walked the aisle of the plane as we flew over inky waters and tried not to freak out. Ordinarily flying is relaxing, but it had suddenly dawned on me that not only did I have no experience with the micro-lending topic I would be teaching in Mongu, but I was also thousands of feet over the middle of the Atlantic with no land in sight for hours. What good was my survival backpack of protein bars and cheese crackers if we never arrived in Africa in the first place?

I went back to my seat, pulled out a book and got a grip. We landed in Johannesburg where I got into a tussle with security guards going through my carry on and taking the batteries I was bringing to the Sisters out of the bag as quickly as I could put them back in. When we arrived in Lusaka, I retrieved my two checked bags with 100 pounds of uniform shorts and freezer bags full of pens and markers for Sr. Grace's school. Upon arrival, we realized that we had no contact information for Sr. Dot, but thankfully she was there waving at the gate in a swirling long teal skirt and white top.

We slept soundly in Lusaka, and the next day we departed on an eight-hour bus ride through the baking bush lands, on black asphalt roads that had been rolled out like cookie dough with ragged edges overtaking the floury beige dust. Waves of dry heat distorted the sparse trees in the distance as we bounced along with no air conditioning while a Nigerian soap opera played on the video. When the bus stopped for a quick break, we were besieged by villagers selling brightly colored bottled drinks and hard-boiled eggs skewered on sticks that bobbed outside the bus windows.

The OK Restaurant greeted us upon our arrival in Mongu. Entrepreneurs were everywhere—setting up shop in little corrugated buildings of ultramarine, scarlet and grass green, selling block stamped fabrics, pastel plastic housewares from China, and Mongu rice harvested from the red iron-rich soil piled high in dark burlap bags.

We were staying in the compound on the outskirts of Mongu with the Sisters of the Holy Cross. They were a German order, and many of the Sisters had lived in Mongu for more than 40 years. The simple single-story concrete buildings circled a chapel building surrounded by carefully tended flowerbeds. The crown of thorns cacti that were houseplants in St. Louis grew three feet high in Mongu, serving as a bramble fence around the property.

It was the dry season, and the heat was unlike any I had experienced during the humid St. Louis summers. Our simple rooms had a single bed and a desk. We had two fans for five people, and two of the other women needed the fans more than I did. All of the bathroom fixtures were stained deep copper red from the heavy iron deposits in the water and I noticed that the Sisters' fingernails were tinged with mineral traces. Bottled water was the norm although the Sisters did have an elaborate system for distilling the iron from the water so that the water was useable for other purposes.

Sr. Grace met me at the door and insisted that I rest. I gave her the uniform shorts and she was also quite interested in everything else I had packed. Before leaving for my trip, I had gone to Mexico City for a meeting where I had dinner with Sr. Leticia Rodriguez Hernàndez, CCVI. Sr. Leti was stationed in Zambia but had come back to her native Mexico for a visit. I asked her what I could bring the Sisters as a special gift, and she had replied, "Maseca for tortillas." I had two five-pound bags of that flour in my rolling backpack for the Mexican Sisters working in Zambia. I gave Sr. Grace the pens and markers for the school along with 100 pounds of navy-blue uniform shorts.

The morning of my presentation dawned, and I prepared the simple conference room for a group of Lozi tribeswomen so that they could begin their micro-lending circle. The women arrived in bright batik wrap dresses that were every shade of the rainbow. One woman had lost her home to a fire in the past week. Many had seen family members die from AIDS. All lived within limited means.

Despite this, the women were happy and optimistic. They had recently formed a rice collaborative to capitalize on the iron-rich rice crop of the western province and had been given land to farm by the tribe. Women holding the land was a rarity and they were excited about the prospects for communal farming. They were born entrepreneurs.

Sr. Dot left me there to go meet with the rest of our delegation who were teaching early childhood development that day to the teachers from the local schools. I was on my own. We sat to begin our circle. They spoke Lozi. I spoke English. The handouts made great scrap paper. Sennnana, an Oxford-educated princess of the tribe, served as our translator and I made a quick decision to discard my presentation. I began asking questions:

Why did they want a micro-lending circle?

What could the funds be used for and what projects fell outside the circle?

Who could participate and how would decisions be made?

What was the amount of the loan? How long could the loan last and what was the interest?

The women had their own circle process. For each question they would start at a different point of the circle and go around. All decisions were made by consensus. The reason for micro-lending was simple: They wanted to start businesses. That should have been obvious to me since the entire town was given over to small entrepreneurs. Funds could be used for micro-enterprises, for their children's education fees, and for funerals, but not for bottle stores. They had a bit of a debate about the interest rate, and finally settled on five percent. They quickly settled on loan terms. In the end, they were so efficient that they completed the micro-lending design process in the morning and took the afternoon to develop their business plan for their fledgling rice business.

At the end of the day they danced, swaying rhythmically around the circle in time with the cadence of their lilting harmonious song. The affirmation and empowerment of that day I carried back with me. When I returned to St. Louis, I shared this experience with several groups that worked with women in the community to see what interest there might be in micro-lending in my home community.

Sharing what was learned in Mongu provided inspiration for the micro-lending work of the Women's Helping Hands Bank in the Forest Part Southeast neighborhood. Under the leadership of Bobbi Sykes, the women in that neighborhood replicated the micro-lending model of the Lozi women of Mongu. While the communities could not be more different in some aspects, they shared a love for their neighbors, years of trust and mutual support, and the shrewd wisdom and practical common sense that have been the bedrock of women's relationships. As Bobbi often says, "Banks do a credit check. At the Women's Helping Hands Bank, we do a face check."

# Nalikwanda: Finding a Friend

Toward the end of my time in Mongu, I spent the day with Sr. Rosa Margarita Valdés, CCVI. She has dedicated her life to being a missionary, and I could see where her friendliness, warmth, sparkling brown eyes, and engaging smile could establish a sense of connection wherever she went. We were about the same age, and since she had studied English prior to coming to Zambia, we could compensate for my nonexistent Spanish and talk a bit.

That morning I helped her load the small dusty truck with infant formula to take to the clinic. Crown of Thorns cacti hedges delineated the driveway from the dry red dirt. Sr. Rose Marg was working with the mother and infant program. At the clinic, mothers with AIDS or who were HIV positive came for medical care and formula so that they would not pass the infection to their babies. Today was a clinic day for the women and children. I hopped into the truck and we were on our way, leaving the whitewashed compound of the Holy Cross Sisters on the outskirts of town and taking the rutted road out to the paved main thoroughfare.

Almost everyone we passed was walking barefoot on the burning pavement. Many of the women were carrying heavy loads—fifty pound bags of Mongu rice, water containers, large baskets—on their heads and I was amazed at their calm strength and how impervious they were to the stifling dry heat. We passed dozens of tall cashew trees growing on the side of the road along with the mangos that grew everywhere. As we drew closer to town, we saw open-air markets and small shops selling household goods, fabrics, fishing nets, alcohol, and clothing.

Sr. Rose Marg and I arrived at the small concrete building that housed the clinic. In the main room, women gathered with their infants and children. A nurse had paperwork on each woman and would dispense the formula for the infant and prescriptions for the mother. As I skimmed the documents, I could see that most of the women had active cases of AIDS. My heart broke as I realized that many of them might not live to see their children grow up. But they were going about life just the same, talking with each other in low conversations in Lozi, sharing a laugh with their children as they played. The nurse suggested we take pictures of the families. The clinic could print the photos and give them to the women. I was happy to oblige and snapped photos of any families who were interested. I didn't keep the pictures because they weren't for me; they were for the women and their families.

When we returned to the convent in Mongu, I noticed a small wooden boat on the mantel in the main room. It was a long canoe, brightly painted with wide vertical black and white stripes and a wide canopied structure in the center. The Sisters had invited us for dinner that night, and Sr. Rose Marg was excited to serve enchiladas using the maseca I had brought from home. I had passed their well-tended vegetable garden on the walk over, but that was no substitute for authentic Mexican food.

While she had always intended to be a missionary, Sr. Rose Marg mentioned that one of the hardest parts was leaving all the familiar things of everyday life behind. In Mongu, there are no coffee shops, parks, streetlights, or movie theaters. Cell phone and internet service can be spotty. I had noticed that myself. Among our group, only one cell phone had reception, and even though I only had been gone a week, it had seemed much longer because of the isolation.

While new experiences were everywhere—new foods, fledgling ministries, even different stars—it was challenging to be limited to being with the small group of Sisters, priests, and international aid workers, and not know the people. I asked her about that little boat on the mantel, with its black and white stripe hull and a small cabin in the middle, topped by an elephant.

Sr. Rose Marg told me that the boat was called the Nalikwanda, the royal barge of the Lozi tribe. The ceremonial barge plies the Zambezi River in formal processions of the Lozi king. This small souvenir was a gift from Joy, a Lozi woman Sr. Rose Marg had met who worked with the orphans. Over time, they became friends. Joy suffered from AIDS and as her illness progressed, Sr. Rose Marg would visit her often in her home. Although Joy passed away, the little boat is a continual reminder of that relationship, and the first friend Sr. Rose Marg had in Mongu.

Our friendship was born that evening in Mongu. Our paths would cross again in San Antonio and Mexico City, at meetings when I'd least expect it. As is the case with good friends, we would pick up right where we left off. Recently, we were together in Peru, where Sr. Rose Marg now works as a missionary. As always, I brought flour for tortillas, crema, and this time, some churro mix. A taste of home is always welcome.

She shared some of what she had learned from the missionary experiences that had taken her to work with the indigenous people of Mexico, to Peru, to Zambia, and now back to Peru:

*I have always been a missionary at heart. It is a unique call. I feel the call and I live it. I am very happy in the places where I have been. My heart is still in Zambia. I first came to Peru in 1985 and left in 1994. Now I am back.*

*In Mexico, I worked 15 years as a teacher and in the indigenous areas in the south of Mexico. Working with the indigenous people in a parish is very different, because you have to learn their culture, religious customs, and dialect. While some of the work the people do in rural Mexico and Peru is similar, the Spanish is different and learning how to speak correctly took time. The religious customs were similar because of the influence of the Spanish in both countries.*

*My first time in Peru, I worked in Cambio Puente. We started a club for the disabled and now that I have returned, I went back, and the club is still there with new leaders. They have a micro-enterprise using sewing and knitting machines they received from a priest. It is so encouraging to see that the people are leading the club, and it is thriving since our Sisters left Cambio Puente five years ago.*

*Now we are working with the families and lay people in the parishes and we are accompanying them on their journey. I see a definite change in the role of the laity since Vatican II. We are closer to them and they are taking leadership. The laity are committed and that strengthens our work and the mission.*

Sr. Rose Marg also reflected on the dangers the Sisters faced in the 1990s when the *Sendero Luminoso*, the Shining Path, a terrorist group, was highly active in Peru.

That dangerous time shifted her approach to her ministry with the people of Peru:

*My time here in the 1990s coincided with the rise of the Shining Path, a terrorist group. The situation became very dangerous. They were murdering the people, and they also targeted priests and Sisters working in the communities. All our Sisters in Peru were living in dangerous situations. We were working directly with the people and the Shining Path perceived us as a threat.*

*Sr. Carol Ann Jokerst was the General Superior at the time, and she came from San Antonio to Peru. She arrived at the airport amid soldiers with machine guns, and came to ask us how we felt about staying in Peru or going back home. She said, 'I have this plastic card right here. We can buy tickets and you can fly home.' She asked us one by one if we wanted to stay or go. Each of us wanted to stay.*

*We were working in Chimbote, in Huancané, and Lima. Some of us were in Cambio Puente. Each of us had a different experience. I was in Huancané. We spent our time responding to the needs of the vulnerable and tried to help people defend their lives. We gave them food and provided healthcare.*

*One of the Shining Path came to my house, and I asked him what he wanted and why they were hurting the people. He told me not to worry, all he wanted was food. However, I knew he didn't just want food. He wanted money. The food was just an excuse. He wanted money for guns and weapons. It was a pretense.*

*The Shining Path would recruit the young people, only the males. They came to towns and villages and killed the others. I went with one of our Sisters to a meeting the Shining Path organized, because they wanted to convince the people that the Shining Path was good and was there for them. We wanted to know what was going on. They didn't know we were Sisters because they assumed most of the missionaries were white. They were always looking for people who looked different. They thought that the white people had access to money and were influential.*

*In Huancané, they were looking for those who worked with the poor. Sr. Grace O'Meara and Sr. Esther Chavez were here. We were so worried, because the Shining Path said the town down the road would be their dinner and Huancané would be dessert. When they came, we went into hiding. A priest was shot, and Sr. Esther Chavez treated him.*

*It was a war. The terrorism is not entirely over. The Shining Path is still in the mountains, jungles, and remote areas. They went underground in the rural areas and in the Amazon.*

*As a Sister, I received a call to serve God and that meant serving the poorest people and most vulnerable, the ones who had no voice. I entered because of that.*

*That was what I had in mind. But when I started to work with the people in Peru and faced the threat of the Shining Path, that changed things. I realized it was not just about serving the people.*

*Because with the terrorism around us, the people needed protection and they needed me to walk along with them. They had rights just like I did, and we were together. The only way to change things is to enter into their reality, work with them, and incarnate the Word. That changed my life. I didn't go to protect, but to walk with them. Walk with their culture, learn their perceptions and how they see life, and make known the Incarnate Word.*

# RE-Barn: The Mission Lives Within

I am a beekeeper. In May, the primary nectar flow is in full swing and my bees are single-mindedly going about their work. Some guard the hive, some fetch water from the pond, forage for nectar or pollen, or alert their comrades to new blooms by dancing on the doorstep. Others hang onto the hive box and fan it with their wings to keep the inner hive cool. All is in service to one mission.

I first met Sr. Alice Holden, CCVI, when she was leading the RE-Barn, a spirituality and arts center in the Congregation's old dairy barn. Sr. Alice is a white-haired woman of wisdom, her features sharp, her eyes kind and laughing. She is a T'ai Chi Chih practitioner, tall and angular, moving effortlessly through the world of spiritual traditions.

Sr. Alice's white barn housed vibrant art and quiet music where the dairy stalls had been. The soaring beams of the hayloft framed a contemplative sacred space. I loved brushing against the tall rosemary bushes as I walked into the barn, reflecting upon artists' visions, listening to Sr. Alice as she frankly shared her latest spiritual journey. But then it was gone.

The Sisters' retirement complex was next door and needed more space. The charming dairy barn gave way for senior apartments to expand the Sisters' ministry to serve older adults. Over the years when ministry needs called, the Sisters had sold off land to build hospitals or support schools. The University of the Incarnate Word covered acres of what had been a land of small springs and live oaks. Responding to the needs of times and ministry remained fundamental.

Still, the loss touched my heart. I thought of Sr. Alice, the scent of the rosemary, the heat bouncing off the Texas limestone that bordered the barn path, the light coming through the square dairy stall windows. A high-rise had replaced the white barn. I could not imagine how terrible Sr. Alice felt about losing that beautiful space.

A few months later I was in San Antonio walking the Motherhouse grounds behind the retirement center. Suddenly, I saw Sr. Alice striding toward me, tall and slender in a red shirt and denim skirt. I closed the gap between us and blurted out my concern for her and the loss of the barn. "How are you doing? What are your plans? I am so sorry..."

She gave me a beaming smile and replied:

*The barn was just a place. It was a gift. A beautiful gift. The last day as we were packing up the RE-Barn, we were closing, and I had no place to go. I called over to the retirement center, The Village at Incarnate Word, and I asked the director if there was a place where I might put up an office. When I dialed, I was connected without the phone even ringing. The director was ringing out to somebody else and got my call instead.*

*I said, 'Hello! Hello! This is Alice.' 'Oh,' he said, 'This is Steve Fuller,' and I said, 'Well, I'm calling Steve Fuller. How are you?' 'Ahhh, fine,' he responded. I said, 'Remember I talked to you about an office downstairs. Is there one down there that I could borrow for a while?' He told me there were two and asked which one I would like. I said, 'Whichever one would give greater glory to God. I think the bigger one.' I moved into the bigger office.*

*Now I have a new ministry, Chispas, or Sparks, which I have named for the sparks of the Divine within each of us. Christa Humana Inspia Su Pasion por las Artes y Spiritualidad (Spiritual Practices and the Arts, Inspiring Knowledge of the Arts and Spirituality).*

She took me to her small, ground floor, windowless office, a far cry from the spacious bright old dairy barn. I saw little touches that made the room distinctly Sr. Alice—colorful folk art from Mexico, rich tapestries depicting village life in Peru, stout pillar candles, a statue of Our Lady of Guadalupe.

*You see, the mission is always within me.*

And I did see. With Sr. Alice, the place is unimportant, because she carries the mission within wherever she is. The mission manifests itself in whatever she is doing. The mission flows through her life and unfurls into the world.

I have thought about that conversation with Sr. Alice many times. So often, we get caught up in the need to possess something, whether it be a place, a project, our job, or another person. To varying degrees these things are necessary for us, but they do not define us. Each of us has a mission. As we grow in the mission, we carry it within.

The bees currently live in a hive box in my yard, but they could swarm and move to a hollow sycamore tree or rotted building eaves. The bees would construct new comb, find new gardens, replenish the honey stores and create a new community.

We carry the mission within.

# Give It to God: Believe

When I tell people I work with the Sisters, they are intrigued. What are they like? Who are these mysterious women? I emphasize that the Sisters aren't a mystery, and they didn't disappear—they are very much a part of our community and are just pursuing other avenues besides teaching and nursing. They are active in social justice, advocacy, and care of the poor. Sisters run St. Anthony's Food Pantry, do home visits with Nurses for Newborns, organize communities through Metropolitan Congregations United, tutor immigrant children in a mobile tutoring center, protest at the Bridgeton landfill, and bring healthcare to Washington County in a mobile clinic. Each one is unique. They have personalities, they have friends, hobbies, worries, and joy.

There are some commonalities, a shared culture that is created by what they would call, "formation." Formation is the underpinning of becoming a Sister. In the past, the formation was cut into distinct segments as part of a seven-year process—the Sisters were Aspirants, Postulants, Novices, Temporary Professed, and then in Final Vows. While the terminology has changed, the Sisters still are part of a process that can take as many as seven years before they make final vows.

These shared experiences give the Sisters touchstones for how to live their vocation, how to relate to others, and how to make decisions. This gives them a special grace to face difficulties with a calm acceptance. That doesn't mean they don't meet a challenge or avoid problems. They are not passive observers of life. They are proactive, but they manage not to become obsessed with worry. That is a quality I envy.

There is a saying that the Irish aren't happy unless they know something bad is lurking just around the corner. The particular curse of being Irish-Catholic is the ability to turn over a problem in your mind so that it becomes a constantly churning undercurrent to the day. I had perfected this affliction to an art form.

Fortunately, I have been blessed to have Sisters who work at the Foundation. Sr. Helena Monahan, CCVI, is one of those Sisters. She is a petite redhead who grew up in North St. Louis. I call her the resident wise woman. She is an attorney with a Ph. D. in English who had been the chancellor of the University of the Incarnate Word as well as a former provincial and congregational leader.

More importantly, she is my dear friend. I couldn't ask for more.

I came to Sr. Helena one day after waking up at three in the morning, not falling back into an exhausted sleep until dawn. I was not in the best of moods and I dumped the problem figuratively at her feet that had kept me tossing and turning. She left her desk and sat beside me. She knew that I had been obsessing over this for almost a week, and that despite all the worry and anxiety, I was no closer to a solution. That in fact, the solution was totally out of my hands.

Sr. Helena told me, "There are times when I have been extremely worried. I would get to the point where it was all I could think about. When that happens, I stop and say to myself, 'Give it to God. Believe. Believe.' I just keep repeating to myself, 'Believe.'"

I tried to take that in, and she could see by the look on my face that I was struggling with how that could really work. In a we-can-do-everything-world, this approach flies in the face of what we are told every day. The idea of turning something over completely to God was totally foreign to me. From my perspective, it was easier to brood and keep worrying. Worry itself had almost assumed a life of its own that was bigger and more important than the actual problem itself.

Sr. Helena knows me too well, and she continued, "I know this isn't easy to do. Whenever the worry surfaces, however, I just keep repeating to myself, 'Give it to God.

Believe. Believe. Believe.' And that actually works. I hand it to God, and eventually things are resolved. I wish I could take this worry away from you. You need to let it go."

I decided to try, and I found that was really hard. Re-hashing the problem from every possible angle, re-peating the series of events in my mind, talking to myself about the problem in my car on the drive home, were all comfortable habits. It was easy. Like knitting, I could do it without even being aware.

"Giving it to God" takes deliberate action. Tamping down the worry, saying, "Believe," turning away, shutting the door on the mantra of worry by replacing it with a new mantra, requires willpower. Worrying is a strong addiction.

Now on days when worry overtakes me, I continue to say, "Believe. Believe. Believe." I still fail at this more than I succeed, but sometimes it works. I manage to quietly close the door, move on with my day. I shift focus and remind myself that every day almost everyone in the world is trying to do good, and that by and large, we are all doing the best that we can.

As Sr. Helena reminds me, Julian of Norwich said more than half a millennia ago:

*And all shall be well, and all shall be well,*
*and all manner of things shall be well.*

# Deep Peace: The Vatican Visitation

Usually, the Visitation brings to mind the Biblical story of Mary and Elizabeth rejoicing in anticipation of carrying new life into the world. For our Sisters, it is a new story, Visitation House. Within the walls of a white-pillared mansion in a San Antonio neighborhood that had seen better days, Sr. Cindy Stacy, CCVI, and Sr. Yolanda Tarango, CCVI, welcome homeless women and children to step toward a new life of compassionate self-sufficiency. The families live with the sisters and the old family parlors are playrooms for happy children. The only thing missing is a yellow Labrador retriever relaxing on the wide veranda, and if I have my way Sr. Cindy will finally take the plunge someday and the vision will be complete.

The Vatican, however, has a completely different concept of Visitation, and in 2012 made a pronouncement that rivaled a tsunami. Formally referred to as, "The Apostolic Visitation of the American Institutes of Women

Religious," ostensibly the process was to "look into the quality of religious life." Quickly, however, other motivations rose to the surface, since the focus of the Visitation centered primarily on progressive orders of sisters and their national organization, the Leadership Council of Women Religious. Cloistered nuns were not the focus. Conservative bishops and cardinals had watched as Catholic sisters worked for social justice in the civic and governmental realm, taking stances that were sometimes at odds with those of the Church's male hierarchy. The Visitation was the response.

Mandates quickly followed under the oversight of a conservative Cardinal and the superior general of the Sisters of St. Francis of the Martyr St. George. The Sisters were to complete individual questionnaires, respond to a lengthy list of overarching questions about the congregation, and to delineate their financial assets. In most cases, this would be followed by personal visits from teams of Sisters from other orders who would conduct on-sight interviews with the leadership of each congregation of women religious.

In St. Louis, the reaction in the heavily Catholic city was immediate. After several years under the authority of a leading conservative prelate, Cardinal Raymond Burke, I thought we had become inured to harsh pronouncements. We had made national news when the cardinal decreed that those supporting Democratic presidential candidates could no longer receive Communion. Three women were ordained at a local synagogue led by a female Reform rabbi and St. Louis made *The New York Times* as the Cardinal declared the rabbi persona non grata and excommunicated the women priests. A dispute between St. Stanislaus Kostka, a historic Polish Parish, and the Archdiocese over the ownership of the church property culminated in the excommunication of the Parish Board.

It was startling to see excommunications coming over the parish fax machine, when I had always believed the process involved men riding on horseback from St. Peter's across Europe in the dark of night, through a world of sealing wax, parchment, and quill pens. The Catholic Church of my pre-Vatican II childhood was staging a comeback, but we weren't all on board.

Suddenly, everyone from the UPS guy to my Lutheran neighbor was telling me how upset they were for the "nuns." Priests pulled me aside to commiserate. Since I worked for Catholic Sisters, suddenly I became their emissary, receiving verbal tribute from the non-Catholic and Catholic world alike. It seemed like practically anyone I bumped into had an aunt, a cousin, or a beloved family friend who was a nun. Overnight, people were overwhelmed with nostalgia for those ruler-wielding women of their grade school days, or the Sisters who sat at the admitting desk of the hospital, or the nuns they had met at the protest rally.

My Irish aunt who carried St. Theresa, the Little Flower, novena cards in her purse stunned me when she confessed, "Bridge, I just can't get over how mean the Archbishop is, but I am too old to become something else." I went to a Catholic Charities luncheon where the Auxiliary Bishop was speaking, and a Jewish judge at my table was busy handing out buttons he had ordered, "I STAND WITH THE NUNS." I noticed that the priest from the chancery at our table did not take one.

It was an intense time. I thought of our office's praying sister, Sr. Felician Borgmeyer, CCVI, who had dedicated her life to working quietly at Incarnate Word Hospital. At the end of her time there, she was assigned to pastoral care and spent her evenings praying the rosary in hospital rooms with the dying. Now in her nineties, her main interests were her house plants and the visions of Mary at Medjugorje. She spent her time at Mass or in prayer.

One day I was called out of a meeting because she was on the phone. Since she had never called the office before, I was a bit alarmed. She had called, she explained, because she couldn't remember if she had sent a thank you note for the flowers we had delivered for her feast day. She thought she had, but just in case she hadn't she wanted to thank me.

The card was on my desk.

The idea that the Vatican wanted her to tell them how many times she went to confession or if she attended daily Mass made me see red.

Then I received the call. The Visitation team was coming to San Antonio next month and wanted to hold a small group meeting with people who worked with the Sisters. Sr. Yolanda Tarango, CCVI, the Congregation's leader at the time, invited me to be a part of it. As the weeks passed, I kept thinking of how outrageous I found the entire undertaking. My Irish temper was in full force as I brooded over how our Sisters had given a century of faithful service and this was the response.

The day to leave for San Antonio arrived. I was organizing what I would take with me when I got the message that Sr. Mary Pezold, CCVI, had called earlier and that I was to call her before I left. I was focused on getting out of the office and decided I would call later, but my assistant was adamant. Sr. Mary really wanted to talk with me.

That struck me as completely out of character. Normally Sr. Mary would not be so insistent. She was a pastoral associate at the largest parish in the archdiocese, St. Joseph's in Cottleville, and universally beloved. Sr. Mary carried a calm kindness within her. She had been my Board chair for nine years and Sr. Mary's wisdom and grace came through in her quiet voice, gentle grey eyes, and patience. She also had a merry sense of humor, a will of iron, and was famous for writing so many thank you notes that we joked she even wrote thank you notes when she received one.

I called her back and she said she wanted to pray with me before I left. I responded that was fine and mentally began going through what I needed to do before my departure. When the prayer ended, I thanked her quickly and started to say goodbye. She caught me, and said, "No, wait. I can tell you are angry about this, and that won't do. You can't go into this with anger because that anger will come through when you are in the interview. This is important."

As always, it was about relationship. And then with calm wisdom, she talked me through what the process might be, how the questions might be posed, how answer might be framed. I listened and relaxed.

As I thanked her, I said, "Sr. Mary, you have a deep peace. I wish I had that deep peace."

She replied, "You have other gifts."

I knew she was right. But that didn't mean I didn't still want what she had, the deep peace she knew was impossible for someone of my impatient, short-tempered, intuitive temperament.

As I was walking out the door, I saw Sr. Mary Margaret, and told her about the deep peace, and how I wished—she cut me off and said, "You have other gifts."

Twice in one day. Perhaps some things are not meant to be, but regardless, I still had some questions to answer in San Antonio.

## Walking to the Grotto

In some ways, the Visitation could not have occurred at a worse time. The Sisters had decided in their previous Chapter meeting to dissolve the provincial level of Congregational governance and flatten their organization. No longer would there be a Mexican Province, a U.S. Province, and a Peru Region with provincial offices and leaders responsible for the day-to-day work of the Sisters in their geography. All the Sisters and ministries would be directly under the Generalate, directed by a Congregational Leader and leadership team elected by the entire Congregation.

Under the best of circumstances, this would be a huge change. For more than 100 years, the Sisters had had a provincial structure, and while the provinces in St. Louis and New Orleans had merged into the U.S. Province decades ago, the multicultural nature of the Congregation had been well-served by the provincial model. Making the change would take commitment and serious energy, but the Vatican Visitation suddenly demanded everyone's undivided attention.

Every Sister had to complete questionnaires. Sr. Yolanda had to fly to Chicago to meet with Mother Clare Millea, A.S.C.J., the Sister in charge of the investigation. A team of Incarnate Word Sisters who had all been in leadership met regularly to tackle the questions the Vatican had for the Congregation at large, relying on the Sisters' constitution, approved by Rome, to craft careful answers. And now the Visitation team was coming to San Antonio.

The day before I was to meet with the Vatican delegation, the Sisters invited me to join them for a prayer service. They gathered at the foot of the limestone steps of their solid red brick chapel, a calm group of older women dressed in light-colored pantsuits and comfortable walking shoes. No one seemed particularly upset or concerned about the prospect of nuns in long habits sent from the Vatican to look under every rock and pebble for a whiff of scandal. It was an ordinary, overly warm Texas day.

I wandered toward the front of the group standing under the facade of the old motherhouse, INCARNATE WORD CONVENT carved in block letters in ivory stone, stained ebony by old roof tar. That motherhouse had been torn down decades before when the ground settled and now only the facade remained, a sheath for their new retirement complex, The Village at Incarnate Word.

I walked back and saw Sr. Yolanda wearing a brightly colored jacket. She was in happy conversation with several Sisters, gesturing with animated flourishes as she laughingly shared a story. Sr. Martha Ann Kirk, CCVI, with her waist-length faded strawberry blonde hair and twirling skirt moved nimbly, organizing the procession. The Sisters quieted, passed out the prayer sheets and formed two lines. As we headed toward the grotto in loose formation underneath pecan trees and live oaks in the parched San Antonio heat, the Sisters began to sing an old hymn.

The reedy soprano notes were a backdrop for reflection as I turned to my right and glanced at the gaudily painted Victorian fountain where a white iron heron lifted its orange beak to the sky and sent the water dancing to the small pool below. I looked past to the wooden gingerbread balconies of the Brackenridge House where the first Sisters had stood in dusty black robes and surveyed a land of springs, sandstone, and brush that would become the heart of an empire of dedication and service.

I turned forward and could see in my mind's eye a cavalcade of Sisters in black habits, white coifs, and black veils with large red embroidered scapulars—*amor meus*—my love—over their hearts. What had unfurled over more than 100 years seemed preordained as hospitals, schools, and orphanages magically dotted the map of the Sisters' orderly provinces under the benign gaze of mother superiors enshrined in those oil paintings lining the hallways inside.

We were a ragtag bunch compared to the perfect order of another time. For one thing, I'd bet a month of Sundays that no St. Louis laywoman had ever tagged along to the grotto back then. And I imagine the singing was a bit more on key, and in Latin.

The procession slowed and I realized that despite these differences, the Sisters of the past and present were kinswomen, one Congregation. Praying and walking together, celebrating feast days, facing the hardship of leaving a beloved school for one in another state, considering the quandary of selling land to build a new hospital that might not succeed, challenging a bishop who had other ideas about the work that needed to be done, wondering how to reconcile differing views among the Sisters about the future of the congregation. It was the same story. Whether in a whirring black and white silent movie or in shattering technicolor, the call remained. At every point in time, the Sisters answered.

We reached the grotto of blackened sienna limestone where Our Lady of Lourdes stood perched above St. Bernadette kneeling below. The Sisters began to pray. As I watched them speak in unison, I saw Sr. Theresa McGrath and Sr. Neomi Hayes, and thought of them leaving the intense green dripping lushness of cool Ireland as young girls for a dusty arid Texas sun, with no thought of returning to gentle rain and a cup of tea. I saw Sr. Carol Ann Jokerst and Sr. Helena Monahan, St. Louisans like myself, who came because they just knew, had felt a need to serve, and had taken the train to San Antonio and another life.

Several Mexican sisters stood in prayer. Even though the investigation targeted Sisters in the United States, they stood with their Sisters. While the realities of working in the *colonias maquiladoras* of Juarez, in the teeming streets of Mexico City, or in the hallways of a high school in Guadalajara might be a different reality, all of the Sisters past and present shared the transcendent call that had drawn those young Frenchwomen to San Antonio in 1869:

*Our Lord Jesus Christ, suffering in the persons of a multitude of sick and infirm of every kind, seeks relief at your hands.*

When Bishop Claude Dubuis wrote those words in a letter to a Sister in a cloistered convent in Lyon in the 1860s, little did he know what the Sisters of the future would face at the hands of his brother bishops. But perhaps he would not have been so surprised. At the time the congregation was founded, the Church did not support Sisters leaving the convents to work among those in need. The Vatican refused to give those orders of Sisters official recognition until 1900. While they emphasize structure, Catholic sisters also have a long history of meeting needs first and dotting the i's and crossing the t's later. Our Sisters were no exception. On that day, I was right there with them.

## A Burning Candle: All Will Be Well

The morning of my encounter with the Vatican Visitation began like every other morning with Sr. Dot and Sr. Neomi. I woke up to the light birdsong of the magpies in the fuchsia bougainvillea outside my window. I heard the Sisters murmuring morning prayer as I reoriented myself to the familiar bedroom with its simple white wicker furniture. For a moment, it was a day like any other, except that the Vatican interview awaited me that day.

As I wandered into the living room, the Sisters were taking a bit of morning tea. Sr. Neomi was fiddling with an iPad. Her eyesight was failing a bit and Sr. Dot had found a site for the Morning Office so that the type could be enlarged. As I listened, both Sisters continued to pray the psalms and readings together.

We sat in companionable quiet with Miss Kitty lying languidly in the sun as I knitted a blue sock. A peaceful morning. I joined Sr. Dot and Sr. Neomi for our usual breakfast conversation around the table of cheerful blue and white plates and took a heaping helping of glittering fruit salad from the indigo-patterned Mexican pottery serving bowl. We continued to skirt the issue and Sr. Neomi shared the latest news of her Irish family long transplanted to England.

It was time to go. Sr. Dot made a quick trip to her room to pick up her bag. I started to clear the table but Sr. Neomi stopped me and took me into the living room. She lit a candle on the small table by the little shrine of Our Lady of Guadalupe saying, "I will burn this candle all day for you until you return to us. You will be in my prayers."

With that blessing, I left.

During the car ride, for once Sr. Dot and I had little to say. I kept turning the upcoming interview over in my mind, picking up and discarding responses, trying to settle on the one that would stun the Vatican visitors with its brilliance. The discard pile was growing. Trying to hold onto the blessing prayer of Sr. Mary Pezold and the candlelight of Sr. Neomi was not working. I felt that Sr. Dot sensed that if we started talking, I would work up a full head of steam by the time I walked into the Generalate, and so chatting was not a good idea. They were all counting on their lay companions to be appropriate, not angry. I sensed a calmness from Sr. Dot that everything would be fine. She gave me a quick hug and sent me on my way. "See you tonight, kiddo."

Walking into the Generalate, it appeared to be a day like any other. Madeline Stacy, Sr. Cindy's mother, greeted me with her smiling Texas drawl and asked whether I had had a good flight. Bishop Dubuis, ever the jaunty Frenchman, smiled from his nineteenth century photograph, a young man with big plans who slept under the stars in Castroville, Texas. I could imagine him giving me an encouraging wink as I walked past the contemporary adoration chapel where the red glass votive flickered through the doorway.

As I walked down the corridor past the sitting room, I tried to be optimistic. After all, how bad could it be? Usually the answer to that was, "Worse than I could imagine." I tried to focus on Neomi's garden, where she was probably working at that moment pulling stray weeds and trimming the oleanders.

Sr. Yolanda greeted me at the door. Not only was she the Congregational Leader, she was one of our more outgoing sisters, charming but sharp, with a doctorate in theology from the Austin Presbyterian Theological Seminary. Her smiling, hickory brown eyes missed nothing. We had worked together for many years and I was always impressed by her ability to put people at ease while not shying away from difficult discussions.

The conference room had recently been revamped to use for video meetings and everything was stark white and hard edges, the walls, the leather chairs, the blinds adjusted silently with the flick of a switch. It reminded me of a room out of a spy movie. Outside the large windows, I could see the birds in the courtyard garden and across the way, the empty community room.

The Visitors were three Sisters, and I was startled to see that the Sister in charge was a School Sister of Notre Dame. These were the Sisters that had taught me in high school, and I had known them to be strong feminists and mentors. Sr. JoAnn Hanrahan, SSND, popped into my head with her fiery red hair and brisk demeanor. When I met her as a freshman, I was a little awestruck that a woman could have such strong opinions, be so self-confident. There was no coddling in her World Cultures class, just an uncompromising expectation that we would speak our minds and meet her high expectations. I could tell from her expression that she knew I could do the work, and she would brook nothing less than my best.

How strange to see a Notre Dame Sister in a modified habit and veil actively participating in what I found to be an intrusive interrogation. She was a canon lawyer and I wondered if perhaps she had decided that working for the Vatican provided an opportunity to help the Sisters' cause from the inside. I considered it for a moment, and then decided that this was doubtful when she brushed off my attempts at building rapport by playing my "Notre Dame High School alumna cards." Not even the mention of Sr. Mary Ann Eckhoff, SSND, a towering leader in the Notre Dame hierarchy, elicited so much as a smile. This was high stakes poker.

The other two Sisters were both Carmelites in full habit, one in brown and the other in ivory. Both had little to say and looked at the floor rather than make sustained eye contact. Our Sisters did not linger in the room, but I wasn't alone. The Sisters had assembled a team of laity to go to bat for them. I recognized the president of the University of the Incarnate Word, the CEO of CHRISTUS Health, a retired Anheuser-Busch executive, a lay Associate, and a theologian.

My place at the table was next to the Carmelite robed in a soft ivory habit with her yellow notepad on the table. When I sat next to her, she glanced at me and with a small smile, placed her notepad on her lap. During the meeting, she took all her notes under the tabletop as if I planned to copy her paper. Did she think we were back in fourth grade at St. Cecilia's? I wished I could move away but decided that would look suspicious. I looked straight ahead and acted as if I didn't notice.

We began with a prayer that had been written especially for the Visitation, asking Mary for her intercession. I thought of Sr. Felician dedicating part of each day to offering prayers for me. I could picture Miss Kitty lounging in the sunbeams by the votive burning before the calm terra cotta Our Lady of Guadalupe standing on her roses, while Sr. Neomi silently dusted end tables and straightened up *The New York Times.* I could hear Sr. Mary Pezold explaining the process step by step in her gentle but firm voice, walking with me into this moment.

Then came the questions, direct and to the point. Questions about the mission and work of the Sisters. What were our opinions? And then finally, had we noticed any areas that were a concern? Were the Sisters faithful to their call? All of us spoke from the heart about the many ways the mission was not only alive but thriving under their leadership. The sincerity of our testimony was evident. I don't see how the On-Site Visitors could have misunderstood. We were confident in our response.

Afterward, the On-Site Visitors thanked us and said they appreciated our comments about the good work of the Incarnate Word Sisters. That was it. Outside, Sr. Yolanda and Sr. Marinela Flores Talavera, CCVI, the Congregational treasurer, greeted us and invited us back to the Brackenridge Villa for a toast in the ornate Victorian dining room.

We walked back with the Sisters past the pecan trees and up the stairs to the ecru wooden veranda. As we entered the cool entry hall, I glanced at the varnished oil portraits of the early Incarnate Word Superior Generals in the dim light. I had recently learned that Mother St. Pierre had called Mother Ignatius, 'Iggy.' Looking at the formal portraits, I would never have guessed that. Iggy looked rather stern to me.

We gathered in the formal dining room, a masterpiece of carved wood illuminated by a gleaming, elaborate brass Victorian chandelier. It was a relief to be finished with the interview and the atmosphere was celebratory as we poured glasses of wine. We didn't spend much time rehashing the meeting. There was no need. None of us doubted that the Sisters and their ministries were on the right path. It was a happy ending to what had started as a stressful day. And now all we could do was wait for the Vatican response.

## THE CONTINUING SPIRIT: WE ARE FAITHFUL

The Vatican Visitation ended, not with a dramatic denouement, but an unsettling silence. Years went by without any word, the radio silence punctuated by sporadic, vague news stories. Unsurprisingly, the Sisters took it all in stride. Catholic Sisters have a long history of standing their ground where bishops and popes are concerned, even on occasion calling them to task. The Sisters had sent in their response, prayed, hosted the investigative team, and now they could focus on their ministries and daily work. Given how busy most of them typically are, putting the Visitation into a virtual closet and closing the door made sense.

The investigation had begun under Pope Benedict XVI. In 2013, with a puff of cottony, white smoke, Pope

Francis took the reins at the Vatican. The winds had shifted, and the Visitation ended. After a number of delays, the Vatican released a report that confirmed what the Sisters had already known: The Sisters in the United States were living out their vocations with integrity, and their work was integral to the Church's ability to carry out its mission. They were faithful stewards.

Sr. Yolanda Tarango was the Congregational Leader during the Visitation and she shared her thoughts about the aftermath of the Vatican Visitation:

*We are a 'pontifical congregation' and so we ultimately do have accountability to Rome. However, the Visitation got off to a bad start. First, the impetus was the assumption that religious life, specifically in the United States, was going down the wrong path and needed to be investigated. It also came at a time of increasing clergy scandals, which led many to believe that it was an attempt to shift attention to the nuns as the problem.*

*Many of the changes women religious had made were in response to the call of Vatican II for the renewal of Religious Life. Women religious had embraced Vatican II and committed to implement it fully. Yet, there are some in the church who saw Vatican II as a threat and continue to question it and the changes it brought about.*

*Key concerns were our strong stance on social justice issues, the influence of feminism, and the assumption that we did not hold the same priorities as the official Church. However, for women religious, the poor and those suffering because of social injustice have always been the priority.*

*Another issue with the Visitation was the way it was initiated. It was not collaborative. It was announced from above and imposed without any dialogue. The Leadership Conference of Women Religious was not consulted until the announcement.*

From the beginning of the process, Sr. Yolanda was not concerned about what would surface as part of the Visitation. The Sisters' work was firmly anchored in both the Congregational mission and its relationship to the universal Church. They engaged in the process as fully as they could:

*In terms of our Congregation, we were not really intimidated by the Visitation for two reasons. First of all, we did not believe that we were doing anything wrong. Secondly, we could say unequivocally that we have been faithful, and so we did not think anything terrible would come of it. We tried to focus on what we could gain from it. Instead of being angry and defensive, our approach was to consider how this could actually benefit us. And it did.*

*The entire Visitation process, including the surveys and interviews, drew us together as a Congregation. We had just eliminated the provinces to create one level of governance, and even though the Mexican and Peruvian Sisters were not under scrutiny, the Visitation brought us together to reflect on our lives as women religious.*

*Religious Sisters were becoming invisible in U.S. society and the Visitation brought us visibility. It opened the eyes of the laity to see that we were still here, and we received an outpouring of support. Our lay co-ministers also came to our defense. The Visitation was more positive than negative because of this groundswell of support.*

*Catholics began questioning what was happening in their Church. Given the scandals the priests and bishops were facing, people were even more inclined to support the Sisters, whom they perceived as being questioned while the clergy squandered its moral authority. I think that the American bishops also recognized this, especially in light of the strong media support the Sisters received. That is probably one reason why the American bishops did not become very involved in the Visitation.*

Sr. Helena Monahan, CCVI, had just completed her term in Congregational leadership when the Visitation began. Like Sr. Yolanda, she focused on the positive aspects of the experience. From her perspective, the Visitation brought unexpected opportunities for unity and spiritual growth:

*When we first learned of the Visitation, we were angry. And among our good friends and ourselves we spoke that anger out and then moved on. I was one of the Sisters who was called to write the responses. We were a team of former Congregational leaders, Sr. Dot Ettling, Sr. Theresa McGrath, Sr. Carol Jokerst and Sr. Teresa Stanley. While it was quite a bit of work, overall, that was a very positive experience.*

*The questions were primarily historical and concerned what the Congregation had actually done in response to Vatican II. That allowed us to see how we had worked through the changes, addressed the challenges, and supported each other. When one of us could not remember something, someone else did. The story came together from different directions and perspectives. Answering the questions fostered true collaboration.*

*At the same time, the Leadership Conference of Women Religious called for a contemplative approach to all of this, to not be angry but to respond with our truth. We trusted that the truth would get us through this process, as would prayer. We approached this from a place of prayer and peace, as well as faith, that we would get through this.*

*This truly contemplative response was almost a stereotypical feminine approach. I don't think the priests and the bishops knew exactly what to do with it. The miracle of that was that it was sustained;*

*we didn't waiver. Once the Sisters were in that contemplative mode it was almost contagious, and we could share it with each other. We helped each other stay in that mode of contemplation and prayer. We became unflappable. We were all in the same boat and it felt good because we were literally saying, 'What can they do to us?'*

My conversation with Sr. Yolanda turned to what the Incarnate Word Sisters had taken away from this experience:

*The Visitation gave us the opportunity to look at ourselves and to reflect on religious life in the U.S. We realized how much we had changed; we appreciated those changes and agreed we would not want to go back.*

*In the end, we were able to say, 'These are the changes we've made, we've made them in good faith, we're grateful for them, and we believe this is where God wants us to keep moving.' It was an affirmation of post-Vatican II religious life, and a commitment to protect it.*

*Ultimately, the Visitation was a reflective moment for us, an opportunity to thank God for Vatican II. We responded to it in good faith, and we are still responding in good faith. We believe that we are living religious life as we were called to live it, and we are committed to continuing. That reaffirmation of our commitment to the life we share was a great bonding moment within our Congregation and among all the congregations.*

*This was especially important at a time when the affirmation of religious life is not being supported by increased vocations. In fact, part of the rationale for the Visitation was the belief that the lack of vocations was indicative of a problem in Religious Life. Our belief is that 'We may not have as many vocations, but we are serving faithfully, and if that means fewer vocations, then maybe it is in God's plan, not ours. We are not called to be productive; we are called to be faithful.'*

*That was the best gift of the Visitation—having the opportunity to say that we are still serving faithfully.*

# Tea and Tamales:
# A Time to Forgive

Whenever I am in San Antonio, I always try to go to the Chapel. I stop to bless myself from the bubbling holy water in the large Baptismal font and pass through the inner doors and walk past the carved oak stalls facing the center aisle on either side. For a large sacred space modeled on the monastic tradition, it is airy and light. The walls are pale, and the marble columns are shades of rose-veined, cream marble. Pastel reliefs across the back of the sanctuary feature scenes from the Sisters' history, and the flowers of France and Texas are painted in lunettes above the side altar spaces.

No matter how hot it is in San Antonio, the Chapel is always cool. The lingering, mystical smell of beeswax and incense are carried on the light breeze that seems perpetually in motion in the sacred space. In the stained-glass windows in the intimate Eucharistic Chapel in the corner, glittering flowers honoring the Sisters' heritage are captured in the colored glass. The shamrocks of Ireland are there. So are the calla lilies of Mexico.

But one flower is missing. There are no flowers from Germany.

Over the years, I had heard that there were Sisters from Germany. They had worked in the convent kitchens. They were the sewing Sisters. But fewer of them had received advanced degrees, taught in schools, or served as nurses.

Whenever I'd ask about the German Sisters, I'd hear stories about their acts of kindness. Invariably the Sister I talked with would express regret and sadness that the German Sisters had experienced the prejudice that had been prevalent in the United States against German immigrants during the World Wars. That prejudice, and ironically, the response to that prejudice—the need to protect those Sisters from the prejudice of the outside world—marginalized those Sisters, leaving their gifts untapped.

Every day, the effects of prejudice and bias in our world and in daily life confront us. Living in St. Louis, centuries of racism and prejudice rip our community. Whether it was the German Sisters or those suffering the impacts of prejudice and racism in St. Louis today, the impact is inescapable. In this respect, life in a religious congregation is no different than life on the outside. A religious congregation is not set apart from the world, and those who enter it bring their worldview and understanding of others with them. One of the Sisters with an expansive world view is Sr. Rosa Maria Icaza, CCVI.

I first met Sr. Rosie in Mexico City at a meeting on Congregational mission. I was assigned to her small group and was the only non-Spanish speaker there. Unlike larger Congregational meetings, there was no soothing simultaneous translation murmuring through an earpiece. At first, I strained to catch a stray phrase or two in the conversation but after a few hours, I was defeated. I had no idea what we were discussing and started thinking about how many days of this I'd have to endure before I was back in St. Louis where meetings were conducted in English.

During the meeting's break, Sr. Rosie sat down with me, beginning a friendship that lasted until her death a few years ago. She was a study in contrasts. Sr. Rosie was petite, but solid. She had lived in San Antonio for decades, but never left behind her Mexican and Basque heritage. Sr. Rosie was an intellectual, but she also possessed the intuitive wisdom of a grandmother with laugh lines framing her deep brown eyes. Sr. Rosie was kind, but never a pushover. She did not suffer fools gladly.

Completely bilingual, she began our first conversation by asking about my family. I was feeling a bit bereft, but it seemed as if within minutes I had relaxed, the frustrations of only a few minutes ago forgotten. (Her offer to translate for me for the duration of the meetings might have contributed to that as well.) As we chatted, she talked about her own family and growing up in Mexico:

*In my home, my father always thought of the United States as a very wonderful country. We were very Mexican on my mother's side and we loved the dances, the food, and Mexican family life. My father's family emphasized Spanish, specifically Basque, culture. My father spent a year living in New York and I think that's why he loved punctuality. The value of time. That was very important to him, and so I already was well disposed towards the United States.*

*My coming to the United States was actually the result of the secretary's mistake. When I was a novice, we were the first group after the religious persecution in Mexico that returned there from the United States to finish our novitiate. The decision was made that at least two of us should learn English because at that time everything in the Congregation was done in English.*

*Two Sisters had studied English in Mexico and one of them was named Rosa Teresa. When the secretary wrote the letter, she requested Rosa Maria instead of Rosa Teresa. It wasn't until we requested letters for the passport visa that they uncovered the error. The Mexican Sisters decided not to send Maria Teresa because of her health, but the Sisters in the United States didn't want me to come since I didn't know English. I went to teach in a school in Mexico City when the Generalate called and said that, since the Mexican Sisters would not send Maria Teresa, then they would take me instead. It was all a mistake, but having just made my vows, I was ready to do what God wanted and so I was happy to come.*

That "mistake" led her to serve on the faculty of the University of the Incarnate Word. Sr. Rosie was instrumental in establishing the Mexican-American Culture Center and served on the faculty for many years, educating thousands of individuals to serve in pastoral ministry to the Hispanic community. But life in the United States was not easy, especially in the beginning:

*Thank God, I have always been very positive. My first challenge was to learn the language. Some of the food was difficult. Customs from home, like my close relationship with my godmother, were not appreciated here. When the young Sisters would gather, I was the only one from Mexico. They would talk about their experiences growing up in Ireland. I didn't have anybody to share with and what I did share didn't have any meaning to them. I would make tea, and they were very critical of that because I didn't make it the way they did.*

*Little things like that add up. It was hard.*

*The Congregation is in the world and reflects the world. I mean, some people would ask you if you eat tamales every morning. The movies and popular culture portray Mexicans as dirty and lazy. We are not like that.*

*Some people would tell me that I don't look Mexican and I said, 'Well how am I supposed to look?' It's just a lack of knowledge and prejudice. I believe the more we interchange the better we will be. We need to learn each other's language and we need to learn each other's values. We will probably find we have the same values but perhaps not the same priorities. We look at things differently.*

*I've examined my own prejudice. When I began teaching, I was very strict and sometimes they tell me a little mean. I was seeing everything from my own perspective which was shaped by what I had learned. I didn't understand, for example, the Mexican-American sisters, because when I was a child in Mexico, we thought of Mexican-Americans as 'wetbacks' who crossed the Rio Grande into Texas, and that they didn't have any manners. I have learned from them and realize that they are people of great endurance, with a great love of their own culture and great love of their own spirituality.*

*Their Spanish is not the same as mine. I was very hard on them, because in their language they mixed Spanish and English when they spoke. Finally, I realized that to speak is to communicate, and if I communicate in both languages together, why not? I also learned to appreciate that they have kept some of the expressions of 16th century Spanish.*

*I grew in love for them and I think that's what we're all about. To be open, to learn different things, to appreciate variety and differences, to learn there is more than one way.*

Over the years with the Sisters, there have been moments when the prejudice that Sr. Rosie talked about bubbles to the surface in offhand comments and small moments that illustrate the struggles that the Congregation and the world still face. Moments like a former Sister telling me that the reason a Catholic Hispanic elementary school is struggling to stay open is because "they don't value education," when in reality it is because the tuition is out of reach for many families. I think of a Mexican Sister recalling the time when she was appointed to an institution's Board, and a non-Hispanic Sister from the States mentioned that she should "dress appropriately."

As one Mexican-American Sister told me recently:

*Yes, there was discrimination in the Congregation towards Mexican-American women and Hispanics. I remember, as a young Sister, the older Sisters would go out of their way to encourage the Anglo and Irish younger Sisters to accompany them in mission and career. I remember being overlooked.*

*Yes, it hurt, though I found a way to support those chosen. I also noticed that those in the small group of Mexican-Americans that entered kept leaving. I remember a Sister friend saying to me in a conversation, 'Sister, I think it is pretty unconscious on their part. You just came from a privileged family— welcome to the real world.'*

*I did have to fight for my specific ministry and education. It was assumed that we were not smart. I do think it was unconscious on the Sisters' part, though at the time I thought there were some mean people in the order. The most hurtful thing for me was that they seemed to not know my name. They would confuse us, and all we could do was laugh about it to hide the anger and pain. This was only some Sisters, however, and I learned to seek out other Sisters who seemed to understand. The connection for me was, and is, the deeply spiritual foundation of the Incarnate Word that I found in myself and others. And there were some peace and justice Sisters that made a huge difference in my life.*

I've reflected on my own views, what I was taught in school, how living in St. Louis has shaped my attitudes and biases. Working with a multi-cultural Congregation is a wonderful opportunity to confront those prejudices, acknowledge them, examine them, and throw them away. I think about how in high school we were told that studying Spanish was for the "C" students, and the "A" and "B" track students took French or Latin. I remember Sr. Rosie and how she could move effortlessly between two languages, and how utterly useless my smattering of French—which consists of asking, "Where is the library?"—was in Congregational meetings. What is the ripple effect of that denigration of another culture? What other assumptions arise from that? How does it foster an assumption of superiority? What do we gain when we set the old paradigms and prejudices aside and open ourselves to the beautiful reality of the diversity of human experience, when we open ourselves to the Incarnation?

As Sr. Rosie said:

*When the superiors here decided that instead of learning English and going back, I should get my degree in Spanish, stay in San Antonio, and teach Spanish, it was a major change in direction. Our charism—to incarnate the love of God—is to be open to God's will. The Incarnation is revealed in human beings and in events that happen in your life. That's where God is. That's the way I saw it. There were hard times when I experienced prejudice and felt alone. That's when we need to examine our response and ourselves. We can change ourselves. We can't change others. We can give them the opportunity to change but they have to make the decision. And even when it is hard, we forgive them.*

*And with that forgiveness comes something important.*

*Interior peace.*

# Open the Tent Wide:
# Welcoming the Laity

The life of a religious congregation is a story of continuing renewal. The Sisters have a keen sense of responding to the needs of the times, and the wisdom of the past informs the work of the future. Perhaps it is the intervention of the Holy Spirit, but it seems as though when new skills are needed, a woman joins to answer the call.

I first met Sr. Miriam Bannon, CCVI, two decades ago before she entered the Congregation. She was a missionary working with the Sisters. She's Irish and brings an intensity and laser-like focus to any project. Sr. Miriam has dedicated her life to social justice for the poor and those on the margins. With short curly salt and pepper hair, sharp eyes and a light brogue, her heritage is reflected in her love of dialogue and debate on the issues of the day.

Usually when I'd see her at a meeting, she was working with the Latinx community. Over the years she had become bilingual, enabling her to move between cultures easily and work in solidarity with immigrants and migrant workers.

Several years ago, Sr. Miriam decided to enter the Congregation. We talked shortly before she made her temporary vows:

*My entrance to the Congregation is not the usual one. The tent opened for me when the Sisters made the decision to have a preferential option for the poor in the 1980s. I was focused on the need to work with people on the margins. It was a turbulent time. Archbishop Oscar Romero had been murdered in El Salvador, and Nelson Mandela had been put in prison in solitary confinement. All of this was having an impact on people of faith in Ireland and we were asking questions. I walked on the streets of Dublin to the American embassy in protest against Archbishop Romero's assassination. We had energy, and we were devoted to the justice issues that were close to his heart.*

*I didn't know anything about the Incarnate Word Sisters, but then I had a chance meeting with Sr. Teresa Stanley and that coincided with my growing interests in liberation theology and missionary work. However, at the same time, you see that there is a bigger movement out there towards social justice. You realize that people are justice-oriented and justice-minded from a faith perspective. In Ireland, there's a group called the Viatores Christi. It sounds conservative but it is actually not. Rather, they put liberation theology into action.*

*I was inspired to become a lay missionary through Viatores Christi and through the Congregation. I began with a three-year commitment. When I returned to Ireland, I knew that Incarnate Word was the place where I belonged. I wrote to the Congregation and I said, 'I'm interested in serving long-term as a full-time lay missionary.' That raised interesting questions.*

*Could laity live and work with the Incarnate Word Sisters? Could social justice focused laity work within the institutional Church? In the Church, back then, if you were sacramental and liturgy-focused you were fine, but if you were social justice-focused that was quite different. Friends of mine from Viatores Christi were going out to Chile in the streets on hunger strikes, or out in the marches of people seeking justice. This was difficult for the institutional Church and sometimes for the Sisters, (the latter not because of the social justice focus, but rather from concerns of lay missionaries putting themselves at risk).*

*I decided after listening to our Sisters' story that I would work with Pastoral Popular, which meant working on the margins with the poor. I joined the Sisters' struggles for economic independence within Pastoral Popular. As a lay missionary, I saw myself as a bridge between laity and religious, and I thought the best way forward wasn't so much to talk about it, but to be immersed in the situation and to be a reconciliation factor. All my energy went into building relationships within the Church, even with those with very opposing views.*

*I still hold to this day that there's a huge number of people who are passionate about a faith that is for justice. And that the way forward is to network, and to reflect the Christ we see in them, to reflect the commitment we see in them. It's not to bring the commitment, it's to reflect it, and to show what's underneath there, what is already within them.*

Sister Miriam served as a long-term missionary for decades with the Incarnate Word Sisters until the program ended. Then she had a decision to make:

*Okay, so that brings me now to today. When the Sisters decided that we were closing the long-term missionary program, they said, 'You can stay on as a lay missionary, or you can leave. It is up to you.' At first, I decided for about 18 months to stay on, but I realized that this wasn't just about doing something; it's about doing something together. I had originally committed to the Incarnate Word Sisters, and I wanted to be faithful to that journey. It felt arrogant to just up and walk away. I was more inclined to sit, have a glass of wine and share stories. Visionaries like Sr. Dot Ettling and Sr. Maria Luisa Velez had opened up the Congregation to a lay dimension and created a path for lay missionaries to embrace both the spirituality and the mission. I decided, 'we either do this thing together or we don't do it at all.'*

*So, when I came into the strict structure of the pre-novitiate and novitiate, I learned about things from the inside and how the Sisters define themselves, but I realized that over the past 40 years religious life had changed dramatically. It really is walking together on a journey.*

*The theologian, Sr. Sandra Schneiders, IHM, points out three main tendencies or motivations for religious life. One is spirituality—everything to do with your relationship with God, another is community— wanting to work together, and the third is mission. Our Sisters integrate these three motivations, although often one tendency may seem to dominate depending upon the individual Sister. The missionaries were drawn to the mission dimension, obviously, and the lay Associates to the spirituality. Our Incarnational charism leads to the community aspect. All three are important. The mission aspect is what originally drew me in, but I am seeing the importance of the others.*

As we continued to talk, Sister Miriam left me with a reflection on the future:

*As I look to the future, I know there's a bigger tent out there, and all of us are quickly becoming aware of the bigger tent. The bigger tent is the whole movement*

*in the world towards care of creation, towards care*
*of the environment, towards social justice, towards*
*interdenominational unity, towards people of faith*
*of all religions coming together, entering into*
*relationship. At a certain point, I believe we will be*
*asked to leave our tent and join a different tent. I see*
*opening the tent as big, as a collaboration with the*
*laity tent. Things will continue to be different, but I will*
*be on fire with the mission.*

*Widen the space of your tent,*
*extend the curtains of your home, do not hold back!*
*Lengthen your ropes; make your tent-pegs firm.*
*Isaiah 54*

I have experienced that widening of the tent as well. When working on a project, it is easy to think that you can do it all yourself. How many times have any of us said, 'I'll just do it myself?' However, when I think of the most successful projects the Incarnate Word Foundation has undertaken—STL Youth Jobs, St. Joseph Housing Initiative, Art Place, Aging Out of Fostercare—in every case by opening the tent, the project took on a new life. The work was much better, and the mission fulfilled much more quickly. Others bring new knowledge, a different perspective, and new relationships form. Those relationships provide creativity to address challenges, awareness to tailor the project to the needs of those who will benefit, and encouragement when you are tired and want to give up.

The Sisters have let me into their tent again and again. Sometimes in obvious ways—when I started at the Foundation or was invited to serve on a committee for a Congregational project. Other times, the tent opened more subtly, when Sr. Dot invited me to stay in her home instead of alone at the Generalate, or when Sr. Rosa Maria Icaza shared her memories of her family and Basque heritage. The open invitation takes the courage to reveal yourself and in return is liberating because you are no longer on your own, but are part of a community within a tent open, waiting for others to come in.

# Jeremiah Calls Me: Living a Mantra

Sr. Mary T. Phelan, CCVI, is one of the many Irish Sisters in the Congregation. She is calm and centered with that trademark Irish brogue. Her resolute spirit breaks free of the infirmities of the bad back that bedevils her and curtails her active lifestyle and pastoral work. She is kind, but also strong and pragmatic. She has the gift of integrating Scripture into her words and her life. When you are with her you know that she sees living as a blessing.

Whenever we talk, she invariably brings up a verse from the beginning of the Book of Jeremiah:

*From before you were born, I knew you.*
*From before you were born, I dedicated you.*
*Jeremiah 1:5*

As she said, "This is the special background music in my head." It is her personal mantra.

I stopped by to have a quick lunch with her in the café at The Village, the Sisters' retirement community. The small restaurant reminded me of a La Quinta hotel lobby, with light matte-finished earth-tone tile and small clusters of coffee shop tables and chairs. In her prime, Sr. Mary T. had been a tall, imposing woman, and as she approached, hunched over her walker in a bright red jacket, I could see the pain of her perennial back problems in her face. But she is undeterred, brushed off my concerns matter-of-factly, and began to reminisce:

*After I graduated, I served as an elementary school teacher in a Catholic school on the west side of San Antonio for 12 years. After teaching for three more years, I spent the next 25 years in parish ministry while also doing vocation work for the Congregation. Providentially, my parish experience took place in Hispanic parishes in both San Antonio and the Rio Grande Valley on the Texas/Mexico border. That made a big difference in my life and I felt it was my calling.*

*At the General Chapter meeting of our Sisters in 1984, we became more conscious of the needs of women and children. The decisions that grew out of the meeting led to opportunities to pursue ministry in underserved areas.*

*At this meeting, we formally adopted the preferential option for the poor. As a result, many of the Sisters chose to work not just in ministries of the*

*Congregation but in parishes, justice and peace work, and in many forms of pastoral outreach. We recognized the need to be in solidarity with the poor who had no one to speak for them. Many Sisters did advocacy work. They attended rallies and protests to oppose the bad treatment given to immigrants coming across the border to the US. We worked on-line and in person.*

*Many Sisters did things quietly on their own, too, but never tooted their own horn about it. In the US, we founded new ministries—Visitation House, El Puente, and Women's Global Connection, and others—all to respond to this new call. And I found my call to do parish work. Sometimes I was not supporting the Congregation financially when I was doing that work. That's always a concern. But our leadership team gave their tacit permission for me to carry out the charism in this way.*

*When I worked in the parish, I often worked with teenagers. I remember preparing the girls for their Quinceañera, a Latino tradition where girls have a church ceremony and celebration upon the occasion of their fifteenth birthday. The priest had delegated this responsibility to me. The event is like a wedding in a way, fifteen young women and fifteen young men are attendants. The entire ceremony is about an hour long and includes singing, Scripture, and blessings. In one particular part during a time for reflection, I used the Scripture verse from the Book of Jeremiah:*

*God said, before you were born,*
*I knew you. From before you were born, I dedicated you.*
*Jeremiah 1:5*

*I used this quote to encourage them to see how, 'Even before you were born, even before your parents met, God had dreams for you.'*

*And the more I meditated on that, 'From before you were born, I knew you. From before you were born, I dedicated you,' the more it became my personal mantra. Then came the questions: I am dedicated for what? I am God's dream for what? The answer came to me: For God's agenda.*

*So how do I find God's agenda? God's agenda could be found in Scripture, in St. Paul's letter to the Corinthians: 'God is love. Love is patient.' Okay. Love is when I am patient. Love is when I am kind. Love is when I'm not puffed up. And so on. That's comforting, God's agenda. But where do I get the strength to do God's agenda? And then the answer came to me that I get that strength from community.*

*The strength comes from belonging to a caring, loving community. I receive strength from community on Sunday in worship when all the community members walk up to the altar, put their hands out and receive from the table. We receive the nourishing food of God, the nourishing food of the Eucharist. To me that is how one gets the nourishment and strength to do God's agenda. Conscious of the fact that I was talking to teenagers and hoping that the ceremony would make an impact, I encouraged them and their parents to see Sunday Mass in community as a place where they would find friendship and acceptance.*

*I am several years now at our retirement center, The Village at Incarnate Word. This mantra, "From before you were born, I knew you. From before you were born, I dedicated you," helps me to make sense of all of this diminishment that I'm experiencing.*

*Of course, there are days when I get frustrated. One of our dear sisters was walking down the hall the other day and said to me, "Straighten up!" This sister is 93. Without batting an eyelid, I retorted, "Sister, I am in agony. I don't need this right now." It just came out. I know that we respect each other, but it would have been nice if she hadn't put it that way and I did not say that back. The blessing is that it wasn't even something for which we had to seek forgiveness. We just laughed and went on and talked about the beautiful sunset and shared a moment that had nothing to do with limitations.*

*I don't use the word, 'handicapped' or 'disabled.' I just use the word, 'limited.' I'm limited in what I can do while I am living at the retirement center. One of my young therapists explained to me that regardless of your level of ability or limitation, you are still going to contribute the rest of your life. And I am working on how I will be contributing. There is a whole spirituality of diminishment and limitation that I want to explore.*

*Sometimes we don't look like we have limitations. I may not look like it, but the limitations are there. The doctor's worry is that with time I will be even more bent to the ground. That's his concern, which is interesting, and I never really thought about that. I only think of going forward and just standing maybe just a bit straighter tomorrow, and with time standing straighter still. It is just an awful cross to bear at the moment.*

I learned later that Sr. Mary T. had been keeping in touch with a friend of mine who had similar back issues—offering prayers and encouragement to help my friend through a difficult time. She was still dedicated, still a part of God's agenda, an agenda of love.

Sr. Mary T. concluded by saying, "Someone mentioned to me, just the other day, that there is a spirituality related to balance, an innate balance in the world. There are always going to be some people who are well and some people that aren't. The way the world is made, there are some things about that balance that need to happen. It's just interesting. I'd love to explore that."

And I told Sr. Mary T. that I'd like it if she were on the well side of that balance.

"Exactly," she said with a grin.

# Deep Waters: The Interior Life

I was relaxing on the stone porch of my daughter's house in Nashville. Mr. Gypsy, the neighborhood grey and black tabby cat was on my lap taking in the early fall sunshine. I am not much of a cat person. Dogs are my first love, but there was something about Mr. Gypsy that was irresistible. He was a contented cat, lolling on my lap while I scratched his ears. Then my phone rang, and it was Sr. Tere Maya, CCVI, with some bad news.

My friend, Sr. Dot Ettling, CCVI, had suffered a stroke. She had been home alone while Sr. Neomi recovered from a broken hip at the rehab center and was now at the hospital. They would call when they knew more. It was so hard to believe. I had been in San Antonio just a few weeks ago, and Sr. Dot had been caught up with concern about Sr. Neomi's frailty, not her own. She had even called me on her way out of town to make sure that I had taken Sr. Neomi to replace her cell phone so that she was not isolated while Sr. Dot was gone.

It never dawned on me that Sr. Dot, who was always going a mile a minute between teaching, directing dissertations, traveling to Colombia for CHRISTUS, and beginning her new work at the University of the Incarnate Word's Center for Global Leadership, would be struck down by a stroke.

Then Sr. Mary Kay McKenzie, CCVI, called. She had known Sr. Dot since kindergarten. They had gone to Incarnate Word Academy together and then on to the convent. Neither one of us could get our heads around what was happening. I knew Sr. Helena Monahan, another of Sr. Dot's classmates from the Academy, was in San Antonio and I decided to give her a call.

As it turned out, she was with Sr. Dot in her room at the hospital. It appeared to be good news. Sr. Dot was doing better, and she wanted to talk to me. I asked her how she was, and although her words were a bit slurred, she told me she was going to be fine. She talked a bit about a meeting she was planning to attend in Heidelberg, Germany for the University of the Incarnate Word, and that she would have to change her flight from Tuesday to Wednesday of the following week. I thought that it was highly unlikely the doctors were going to let her go to Heidelberg but did not say so.

Then Sr. Dot turned the conversation to me and asked about how things were going in Ferguson. A police officer had killed Michael Brown just a month before, and St. Louis had been dominating the national news as people took to the streets to protest his death and the racism that had festered for decades in St. Louis. Since Sr. Dot had grown up in St. Louis herself, she was keenly interested. We did not talk long because she needed to rest. After we hung up, I was so relieved that she was going to be okay. She might need to slow down, which would be hard, but at least she would be okay.

I was wrong about that. The same day as our conversation, Sr. Dot had another massive stroke. She died about a week later. The Sisters were devastated, and so was I. Several of the Sisters had known Sr. Dot since childhood or gone to high school with her. She had the charismatic personality of a visionary and losing her was not just a personal loss for the Sisters, it was a blow to the Congregation itself. She provided so much wisdom and guidance to the overall Congregational direction.

I had been with Sr. Dot at the Bretton Ridge house about a month before and we had a long talk. She was always a proponent of collaborating with the laity and believed that everyone had a vocation. However, this time, our conversation went deeper as she described the meaning of vocation, not only for the Sisters but also for people drawn to work in ministry:

*I always go back to the beginning. What was the inspiration? What guided all of this? I can only speak for the 140 years we have been around, but what inspired our Sisters and the ministries emanated out of religious life. Obviously, one part of that was always the desire to serve, and not to sound trite, but to make the world a better place.*

*I always go back to John 10:10, 'I came that they may have life, and have it to the full.' To me, that is the story of creation and the story of Jesus. We've all been created to have a full life, a human life. Religious life was people's sense that this was their calling, a way to respond to God. Then they saw that they might do things that would enable other people to have the same experience. In simple words, to serve, or to make the world a better place, or to create more justice.*

*I came to religious life because I felt it was a way to draw closer to God. There was sort of a longing. Then the second piece was to be able to serve in some way. I did have a desire to make things better for people who were left out or who didn't have the opportunity. From a very young age that was instilled in me—take care of the one who wasn't taken care of. All of those things, in some very idealistic way, would have led many of us to join religious life.*

*And my suspicion is that it is not any different today, that you and all the other people that are associated with us have a longing for God, or to follow God, or to be more spiritual. They might not even know how to talk about that, but the people working with us want to be better people. Secondly, I think they might want to see more people have a better life, or a more just life, or have a more peaceful life. The motivation is the same as it was for us as it is for the laity that are attracted to us or are attracted with us to the mission.*

As Sr. Dot reflected further, she shared her thoughts on the longing we have for an interior life in order to have deeper spiritual connections and meaningful relationships:

*So, if I translated that to today. I think people today are longing for the same things. The opportunity to have a deeper interior life, to feel and to experience a connection with what they think is their inner-self—their core. Some would call it a connection with God; others would call it the opportunity to grow spiritually.*

*That same thing that nurtured us when we began, the development of an interior life, we have to find ways to nurture the people that come to serve in our ministries. That way it's not only, 'Come and do good works,' or 'Come and be about justice,' or 'Come and be about helping the marginalized,' although I think that's very real. It is also about, 'Come and grow yourself as a deeper spiritual person, come and know God in a deeper way, and come and know the beauty of God within you, in a deeper way.'*

*I think that is even true of young people today, that there is a longing for that among all of us. We probably had more opportunity as young people years ago to develop an interior life than young people do today. I did not live in a world of constant noise and distraction. Obviously, I wasn't living in a quiet world and having reflection and silence all the time, but I had moments of that; I had times that I had experienced the difference. I don't think many young people today even know what that means. It's hard to grow closer spiritually without some opportunity for that.*

*One of the things we cannot lose sight of is the deep formation that the Sisters had, the development of that interior life. Whatever that means today, we have to find how that can be translated into today's world. We have to bring that to the picture. We can't do anything without involving people. You don't do it for them; you don't plan it here and say, 'Here it is.' You have to engage them in creating it. Given the chance to voice that, and then to sit in an experience and have it, they will ask for more. At least, that's my experience.*

*We need to build in what I could call, for lack of a better word, the reflective capacity, or the reflective possibility, to examine what is going on in my life. 'I had this experience, what did it mean to me?' Whether it is reaching out to people, a moment of prayer, a moment of silence or a moment of listening to something, or watching a video, it is the opportunity to ask, 'What does this mean in my life?' We need to build in those opportunities because they do not happen naturally for people today. We move from one thing to the next.*

*Television is a perfect example. The idea is that more information is going to change you. I think what we know now is more information doesn't transform you. More information, without reflection or without integration is not useful. It's not integrative; it doesn't really move you towards a new understanding. Yes, very intuitive and bright people might be able to do this on the fly, but in general, you need practice. Reflection is a skill and an art.*

*We need to build concrete opportunities where people have the experience of reflecting together, of learning together, of being taken out of their comfort zone—maybe to a new place, a new engagement, a new experience, even something that they might not agree with, or they might feel adverse towards, While we are doing that, we need to provide those opportunities in a way that there's an element of safety to them, an element of nurturing and an element of companionship. The point is that there is also an opportunity to develop more deeply as a person.*

*Our charism is clearly built on the importance of relationship, the importance of recognizing we have an encounter here, and that encounter is so precious. That encounter needs to be held. That's why it's so important for us to be involved in issues of health and education for one thing, because those are moments of encounter. Those are real moments when people experience an exchange. When we're learning together and discovering together, that's what I think education is, we're seeing something deeper together. When we're vulnerable, those are moments the relationships are really important.*

*It's also important to realize what it means to be human. There is a human drive to be successful. There's nothing wrong with that. There is a human drive to achieve and there is a human drive to love. Those are basic human experiences, and we need to be present to people in them. Whether it is pain or whether it is joy, they're both real human experiences. Valuing what it means to be human and how to grow as a human being is part of our Incarnational spirituality.*

I had meetings the next day and so did Sr. Dot, and so we decided to call it a night. She ended our conversation with this:

*We'll see each other again. That is one nice thing, Bridget. We have nice visits. Sr. Neomi and I appreciate it and we like it too, so it's not a one-sided thing, you know that. It's part of the relationship, part of the gift of belonging to the community, to the Congregation. That's what we would hope for every single person in all the ministries, that more and more we have an experience of 'we're in this together.' Because frankly no one was ever meant to live in isolation, I mean if we've learned anything from evolution, we learned that. We should have learned it from the Gospel but, frankly, we've learned it from science, too.*

After Sr. Dot died, I knew I would never stay in the Bretton Ridge house again. Sr. Neomi could no longer live on her own and would be moving to the Village at Incarnate Word where she could be with other Sisters. Miss Kitty found a home in Austin, and I would stay at the Generalate the next time I came to San Antonio, which is where I had started.

We never really go back, however, to where we begin.

In the aftermath, I had a new appreciation of what the Sisters really meant when they talked about relationship and presence, of seeing God in other people and in our interactions. Because despite their own intense sorrow, they took time to reach out to me and be present. We grieved together, and in the months that followed, it seemed like whenever I bumped into a Sister, we would share some time talking, remembering, laughing and crying.

*We stand in vigil in this darkness.*
*Dawn will break but it cannot be rushed.*
*This is God's time. Faith will dispel the darkness slowly.*
*God's answers will come gently like Dot's smile and encouragement, like her presence among us.*
*— Sr. Tere Maya, CCVI*

# Trust in God: Solidarity in Peru

In response to the spirit of Vatican II, the Sisters decided to embark on a new ministry in Peru. They have remained there for more than 50 years in times of peace and in times of civil unrest. My knowledge of Peru was superficial, a travelogue of *National Geographic* images of llamas, Incan treasures, Nazca lines, and colorful textiles, capped by the vista of Machu Picchu. In the archives, black and white photos capture the first Sisters cheerfully walking up the stairs onto the airplane to a new beginning. The reality is a lesson in solidarity.

Sr. Rosaleen Harold, CCVI, is a diminutive woman, soft-spoken, with a touch of auburn in her hair. She came to the Congregation from Ireland but spent 33 years working in Peru and was there when Sendero Luminoso, the Shining Path, a Marxist revolutionary group, was kidnapping and murdering anyone who stood in their way:

*I spent more than thirty years in Peru. Each experience has been full of so much grace, but also challenges. There were years in Peru where we were in the midst of a terrorist war during the time of Sendero Luminoso, the Shining Path. I was one of the first Sisters to be stationed in the rural areas and I worked with one of the priests who was martyred there.*

*I had left Chimbote and was working in Lima when Fr. Dordi was murdered. There was such a personal connection with him and the two Franciscans who were killed up in the mountains, Fr. Tomaszek and Fr. Strzalkowski, both from our parish in Chimbote. I didn't know the Franciscans personally, but the Sisters did.*

*In Lima at that time, you were just so exposed. At any time, you never knew when you went out if you would come back. We had car bombs. People infiltrated the parishes from the Shining Path and there was the whole fear of being infiltrated in religious life. At a parish, we found out that a secretary that had resigned was seen with the Shining Path and she had taken some information from the parish files. We supported each other a lot during this time, especially during the terrorist war. We even hid people in our house when the police were after them. Things were that close to us.*

*I can't say it didn't cross my mind to come home. In fact, The Sisters in Peru met with Sr. Carol Ann*

*Jokerst, who was the Superior General at that time, and she was open to us returning home. It was a deep conversation, and the conclusion was: We are not leaving. We are going to continue. And we only had one Peruvian sister at that time, and we wanted to make sure that she felt free not to continue with this if that was her choice. She committed to stay with us.*

*And so, even though it was difficult on the one hand, there were so many graces associated with it, that it was a very deep, spiritual time for us. In a way it was like having a near death experience, you know. I saw what the priorities are. I became much more contemplative. There was a greater integration between what was happening and scripture. Certain quotes from scripture would come to my mind as I experienced certain situations. I felt very peaceful and even though I had moments of fear, it wasn't a paralyzing fear.*

*We opened a formation house for vocations in a shanty town in the northern part of Lima. We went there because we were looking at a new parish. When we came to the area there was a huge banner on the wall on the main street that said, 'Yankees Go Home.' We said to ourselves, it was in one sense an advantage being new, because we were unknown. On the other hand, it was a risk because you didn't know with whom you were dealing. But we went forward and, in the middle of this, even made the decision to open a formation house where our second and third sisters had their formation. Now we have eight Peruvian sisters, a sign of hope for the future.*

*During those difficult times, our prayer became more spontaneous and more connected with what was happening each day. We would pray for specific families who were impacted tragically by the terrorism. It was a time of being constantly aware of God's presence. Everything that was happening made us be more trusting in God. Because you just never knew. I was on a small bus one day and there was some smoke inside. People just panicked. I am the type that I will run if I can, and if I can't, I just keep calm. People started jumping out the windows. It turned out to be a mechanical failure. Anyway, we were very lucky God was with us at that time. I always look back on this as a period of growth that permanently marked my life.*

While times were hard and dangerous, Sr. Rosaleen also recounted the generous hospitality she experienced in working with Peru's diverse cultures:

*In the early days in Peru, we were a community of diverse cultures. There were two Irish Sisters, a Mexican Sister, the first Peruvian Sister, and a German Sister who had worked in the provincial kitchen in St. Louis and at age 72, offered to come to Peru in the middle of all this.*

*When I was working in the rural areas, one of the things that impressed me most was how joyful the people were in spite of the hardships. They were so trusting of a providential God. Even when they lost their crops, there was still a sense of hope. They had a sense of joy, and of course they loved fiesta. They don't have a lot of money, but when it is time for the fiesta, they give it their all. It might be their whole savings for the year. It comes down to hospitality.*

*I remember one time where I went to this very simple home—it was just constructed of reeds from the area—the mother had one egg and she gave me half of it—half of a fried egg and rice. She gave the other half to her husband and he divided that for the children. That is the kind of experience you have with the people. It is just total generosity. We learned so much from the hospitality of the people themselves. They were living Incarnational spirituality.*

# Nuevo Chimbote:
# Beyond Where the Road Ends

In all the years I had worked with the Sisters, Peru was the one place I had not gone. I was finally able to see the Sisters there by traveling with my friend, Lisa Uribe, one of the leaders of Women's Global Connection (WGC). She was working with a group of women who had formed *Mujeres Emprendedoras* in Cambio Puente on the outskirts of Chimbote. The women operate a sewing and knitting micro-enterprise and I was looking forward to meeting them as well.

In Zambia, I had conducted workshops with WGC, but I didn't have any workshop responsibilities with Women's Global Connection on this trip, although argu-ably I am a much better seamstress and knitter than I am a micro-lending expert. This time, I was making the journey to see the Sisters' ministries in Chimbote. Their work had begun with Vatican II about 50 years ago, and the Sisters had served primarily in Puno, Lima, Chimbote, Cambio Puente, and Nuevo Chimbote.

We left the bustle of Lima at dawn and boarded a comfortable double decker bus to go north to Chimbote. I was looking forward to a reunion with my friend, Sr. Rose Marg, CCVI. She had left Zambia to continue her missionary work where that journey had begun, in Peru. The bus took us through flat irrigated fields near the road that were dwarfed by the towering shifting desert sand dunes in the distance. I was struck by the vast distances that reminded me of the deserts in a Georgia O'Keefe painting, the undulating dunes of yellow ochre and taupe shadows set against a light blue sky with a smattering of clouds. It was a quite a change from the vibrant greens of the cosmopolitan city of Lima on the bluffs that hugged the Pacific.

Chimbote is also on the coast. Once a thriving fishing port, the rich fisheries had collapsed due to overfishing and pollution, leaving rampant joblessness in its wake. The city itself was devastated by an earthquake in the 1970s and is still rebuilding. We arrived at the open-air bus terminal and snagged a cab. The music playing when we checked into the hotel sounded like the Bee Gees, and I quickly made myself comfortable in my room with its dim lighting, deep aqua walls, chenille bedspread, and retro 1950s furniture. The sash windows of my room opened into the bright, white-walled main corridor of the two-story hotel with its gleaming tiled floor, tropical plants and scattered seating.

We met up with our translator, Frank, and flagged down one of the taxis that masqueraded as an ordinary sedan that would take us to the convent. The busy city square with its tiny shops and cafés gave way to narrow streets where brightly painted concrete buildings came right up to the edge of the curb. The cab dropped us on the stoop, and we entered through the gate to the paved courtyard of the Sisters' convent. We were greeted by Sr. Pilar Neira Sandoval, CCVI, a Peruvian whom I had first met when she had spent a year in St. Louis studying. Her broad smile made me feel right at home. The convent was simple but comfortable, and I joined Sr. Rose Marg in the kitchen. As I had done in Zambia, I had brought a backpack for Sr. Rose Marg filled with bags of maseca, cans of crema, and churro mixes so that she could cook some delicious meals of her native Mexico. A taste of home is always welcome.

Sr. Rose Marg and I went upstairs to the community room and we caught up on family news as the Sisters returned from their community work. Sr. Hirayda Blacido Enriquez, CCVI, one of the first vocations in Peru, joined us, as did Sr. Maria Marquez Fuentes, CCVI, Sr. Leonila Gonzalez Siller, CCVI, and Sr. Lourdes Gomez Barrenechea, CCVI. The Sisters' ministry in Peru is focused on community. Whether they are providing medical care at Santa Clara Health Center or working in pastoral and social ministries meeting the needs of women and children, each Sister strives to be in relationship with the people.

The emphasis is on community, not institutions. Working in community requires a multi-cultural approach:

*In our work in Chimbote, we recognize that the Incarnate Word lives within the people. The people speak and we do not speak for them. They have their own words and their own voice to speak out on injustice and violence. They have their own culture. Even though we are all Peruvians, we come from many cultures. These cultural differences enrich us and are not a detriment.*

*Wherever we go, the entire Congregation is with us. Our projects are not personal but are of the whole Congregation. That allows us to be brave because we are all together. Our Congregation in Peru is multi-cultural, and the Congregation itself is as well, with a combination of the cultures of the U.S., Mexico, Ireland, Germany and now Peru. We love this blending of cultures. That makes us stronger. In this coming together we have created a new culture for the Congregation in Peru. Working in Peru has renewed our Congregational spirituality.*

*We came to be Sisters to be out in the community. Liberation theology has had a big impact on us and is the reason many of us became Sisters. We want to stand with and help the poorest people. When we went out to Cambio Puente on the outskirts of Chimbote, there was no water, no sewage systems. We collected water in buckets and lived without electricity but by candlelight. Our Sisters there could have chosen to live in a better place with more amenities, but they chose to live with the people who needed them most. We are walking with them.*

*We've had a strong collaboration with the laity from the beginning. We work together and experience the Church as community, not as an institution. We have a strong base in the community, and because the Peruvian Sisters are from that base, we bring an understanding of the cultures of Peru to our work. Our Congregational culture is grounded in respecting others and entering into their reality. We have to leave our preconceptions behind and be open to the process, taking time to listen and establish relationships. Our relationships with the laity are strong and will continue to grow. The people are looking for spirituality and while their spiritual formation is different, we see a strong response from the laity to share our mission.*

The Sisters invited us to go to the celebration they were having next night at Mary, Queen of Nazareth Parish in Nuevo Chimbote as part of the 150th anniversary of the Congregation. Lisa and I had ended our day at San Pedro Cathedral in Chimbote to visit the shrine of three priests who had been martyred in the 1990s by *Sendero Luminoso*, the Shining Path. The Spanish baroque exterior opened onto a surprisingly modern space of white walls and archways framing large oil paintings of saints under the clerestory that extended the length of the nave.

Just to the right of the dome was the shrine for the three priests who had died only a few decades before. They were alert to the dangers posed by the Shining Path but had chosen to stay and share the risks with the communities they loved, far from their native Poland or Italy. For me, martyrs had always lived in the distant past, but these men had lived and died during my own lifetime.

Their large portrait was contemporary, not a stylized oil painting. People literally laying their life down for their beliefs is not something I encounter very often, and it was difficult to comprehend that some of the Sisters I knew back in San Antonio had known them, had lived in Peru with the same death threats, and had chosen to stay rather than return to the safety of home. Sr. Rosaleen Harold, CCVI, had actually worked with one of these priests. Our Sisters had known them during ordinary times and then something cataclysmic had happened.

It was strange to think that I had sat across from Sr. Grace O'Meara, CCVI, at Earl Abels in San Antonio eating lunch and talked with Sr. Rosaleen in the hallway, and everything had always seemed so ordinary, but there was another facet of their lives that had been anything but mundane. People are so much more than they seem.

We left the cathedral for the Congregational celebration and crossed the polished stone plaza with its palm trees to the busy boulevard, but cab driver after cab driver politely refused to drive to the outskirts Nuevo Chimbote. It was too far off the beaten path. I was beginning to worry we would miss the celebration but finally, a driver agreed.

We drove through Chimbote as dusk fell, past brightly lit restaurants, Internet cafés and night clubs. Eventually the highway cut through the desert leaving the lights behind. The few buildings we saw were makeshift, small one or two room homes scattered with just the semblance of a street grid. We turned off the main highway and suddenly the makeshift road ended in the sand.

The driver turned around and said, "this is as far as I can go. The church is straight ahead." Almost like a mirage, Mary, Queen of Nazareth Parish appeared—a large Naples yellow cement church with tall steeples framed against the desert landscape in the dwindling light. It rose majestically some distance away from the humble tiny homes that we trudged past sinking into the dry sand.

When we approached the tall wooden doors, we were no longer alone. The people of Nuevo Chimbote were there to celebrate. Sr. Hirayda and Sr. Pilar lived among them, and everyone was excited to join with the Sisters to recognize their founding 150 years ago in San Antonio at a time when the road ended there, too. The familiar Congregational emblem, celebratory banners, and pictures of Bishop Dubuis and the early Sisters were part of the anniversary display across the sanctuary. The children's choir clustered in front of me in their white choir robes and red sashes, and I was startled to hear a hymn that was set to the tune of the Battle Hymn of the Republic. The blending of cultures can take unusual turns.

After Mass, the people quickly reconfigured the church so that it could be used for the reception. They passed around glasses of *chicha morada,* a sweet drink made from purple corn and spices. I don't believe Mother St. Pierre and Mother Madeleine would have imagined that what they started in a small settlement on the San Antonio River would find its way out past where the road ends in Nuevo Chimbote, but the frontier charism continues as the Sisters go out beyond the paved road to be part of a new community of those most in need.

Sr. Katty Huanuco, CCVI, sees it as a ministry of presence that responds to whatever needs present themselves, exactly how the Sisters began their service in San Antonio:

> *In Chimbote, our ministry has always been about presence. When the Sisters arrived, the people needed special attention. The fishing industry in Chimbote had collapsed. People had come from the Andes region for that work, and their culture was different from the coastal culture. They came to us for help. We worked with youth and children, and began our work in healthcare here. Now the poor families come to us and they come to the Church not just for help, but also for*

*hope. They are always asking for hope. We are helping with necessities. We find them what they need and respond to the specific situation here.*

*Nuevo Chimbote is a growing area. There are many young families there. They need housing and have built tiny homes for their children. The parents work in the agricultural fields. They leave at 3:00 in the morning and work long hours in the irrigated fields. The Bishop of Chimbote talked with us about the needs in Nuevo Chimbote and the priest at Mary, Queen of Nazareth asked us to come work in the parish. We immediately said, 'Yes.' Sr. Pilar and Sr. Hirayda moved to Nuevo Chimbote to live among the people and help them with whatever they need. They have also organized the choir and minister to the families' spiritual needs.*

Months later, I went to Juarez, Mexico to meet refugees waiting at the border. When I had visited the Sisters there a number of years before, they had lived in a simple concrete house on a side street in the midst of the city. Since then, the Sisters had moved, and I found them out past Anapra on the outskirts of Juarez. Their new home is built to be in harmony with the environment, and there is a large community building for gathering with their neighbors for meetings and classes. The yard has enclosures for growing herbs and raising chickens.

The Sisters in Juarez work in *Pastoral Popular*, living and serving the people who are suffering from poverty, the impact of economic globalization, and the violence of the drug cartels. They teach families to attain financial self-sufficiency. They help women to raise chickens to meet basic needs. And when I looked past their new home among the people, I could see that the road trailed off a few blocks away, fading into the desert toward the mountains beyond where the road ends.

# Our Future: A Frontier Charism

Frequently, I am asked how the Sisters see their future. Vocations to religious life in the United States have been declining for decades. Most Sisters no longer wear formal habits and are not immediately recognizable on the street. Some congregations of women religious quit taking vocations decades ago and are moving toward completion, going out of existence. Our Sisters are not in that mode. They are continuing their vocation efforts, collaborating with lay leaders, and responding to the needs of the times.

When we've talked about this, what always intrigues me is that generally, the Sisters don't express much anxiety or worry about what comes next. They are confident that the future will unfold as it should. Their mission will continue because it is a mission they steward, and others also hold that same mission. Their charism, or gift to our world, will live on not only within the Sisters who are still to come, but also in the lay people who work with them.

Sr. Tere Maya, CCVI, sees the Sisters' charism as a frontier charism:

*What does the future look like for the Incarnate Word Sisters and their ministries? 'Oh, my God, I don't have the slightest idea.' It is like being in the clouds or driving in the fog. What are we doing? Our Sisters are not dead. They are not finished. They are continuing to live and to be alive.*

*Our Sisters are searching, doing things together. For example, a Sister in Torreon who is 103 years old and she still goes to meetings. There is vitality. Our Sisters are doing a lot in the world and our Congregation is not dead. The Congregation is alive. We are not a museum. We are a group of Sisters who are called and open to the future. We are always searching, and we are collaborating in that search.*

*We have no choice but to be in a contemplative space. Who has driven through the fog? You hold the wheel. You need silence. You need to focus. We need that focus to engage in a profound listening, to be profoundly attentive to this moment because somewhere something new is happening.*

*How does our Congregational history prepare us for the future? We need to go back to our foundation in order to understand our ministry and mission. When we go back, we see that our charism is rooted in responding to critical human needs. In our story, we have this guy, Bishop Claude Dubuis. You will see him everywhere, and because of him we have a particular style. The Jesuits do things their way, the Baptists respond in their own style, the Franciscans have St. Francis, and we have this guy, Bishop Claude Dubuis.*

*He is not a saint. He is not someone on a holy card. We have a picture of him on a comic book, Claude Dubuis, Priest of the Plains. The Sisters in Houston created an icon of him showing a horse, a gun, and the prairie of Texas, but they also included the Eucharist. We begin our story with Bishop Dubuis with his original letter:*

*"Our Lord Jesus Christ,*
*suffering in the persons of a multitude of the sick and infirm of every kind, seeks relief at your hands."*
*Bishop Dubius*

*We have just finished celebrating that call of 150 years ago. Celebrating the founding letter, the founding call. The world awaits relief at your hands. Your hands and your neighbors' hands are the hands that are called. We bless the hands of all of our collaborators. All 40,000 hands receive a blessing, because those are the hands that are going to respond to the critical needs of today.*

*We have a frontier charism. It is special because most religious congregations in the United States are based east of the Mississippi. Most religious congregations in Mexico are south of Mexico City. We were founded on the Texas border. We went south into Mexico and north into the United States from San Antonio.*

*What does that mean? It meant you were looking out, scouting, going to the edges to see what was going on and what was needed.*

*Our frontier charism is a charism of innovation. We are always learning about ourselves in conversations with others. We were one of the first congregations to create a retirement facility where Sisters live with lay persons. We were one of the first to appoint lay leaders to our ministries. Other congregations of Sisters started that transition only recently.*

*Our frontier charism is a charism of risk and courage. If I look at Bishop Dubuis' story about camping out in the desert under the stars—and our first Sisters' story, arriving on a boat from France—it is about risk and courage.*

*In our own time, things are changing. The Cardinal of Chile met over tea with Sr. Kevina Keating, General Superior of the Sisters of Charity of the Incarnate Word, Houston, co-sponsoring the Congregation of CHRISTUS Health, its ministry to Santiago, and asked why CHRISTUS was there, but not any Sisters. I thought that was a good question and I have no idea what the answer is. What I do know is that now it is our ministries that are going to new frontiers.*

*Our Sisters are behind the ministries on the new frontiers. That is our unfolding story. The Congregation is not about itself. The ministries are not the Congregation's. All of this is about the mission of Jesus. The ministries are the visible mission of God.*

Sr. Walter Maher, CCVI, also envisions a mission on the margins where the frontier is embodied in the rapidly changing dynamics of our world:

*The Congregation is going to be very different in the future. Perhaps it will be more radical because the challenges in the world are greater in terms of poverty, the level of violence, war, and the displacement of persons. Social media is also having a tremendous impact, and not necessarily always in a good sense because it changes how we relate. Here at the University, people would rather text than have a face-to-face conversation. Given that Incarnational Spirituality is in our relationships, we are going to have to be in the world in a different way. Our Sisters may not always be large in numbers, but we will be found in the prophetic part, in the witness part, or out on the margins.*

*If you look at Pope Francis, he often talks about that sense of radicality—about how if we are ignoring the poor then we are ignoring God. This is a change in the Church and this is where Sisters of Charity of the Incarnate Word will be, because Incarnation means being blessed, being present, being in the encounter, being in the dialogue and then determining what the action has to be. That's what we are called to do.*

*If you think back, when we started, we were not nearly as large but were much smaller. Sometimes being large and having established institutional ministries is good, but when we are smaller, we can be freer to move more expeditiously and to respond more immediately to the needs. We also don't always need huge financial resources but sometimes we get that locked in our head.*

*I always go back to those two women, Mother St. Pierre and Mother Madeleine. Whatever they were doing was in response to what the need was, and the resources were always there. We need to think about our resources in a different way. We need to think about the providence and beneficence of God. We need to look toward the generosity of God, and whole notion of the abundance rather than scarcity. When we focus on scarcity, we limit our possibility and our capacity.*

*That is the radical piece. I go back to Bishop Dubuis writing to Sr. Angelique Hiver in the monastery asking for Sisters to come to San Antonio, and she said, "'No, we can't do that. We're monastic," but they figured out a different approach. They went down to the bottom of the hill in Lyon and invited some of the nurses there to come up to the monastery. With*

*that out of the box thinking, they devised a different
strategy. Sr. Angelique trained these women for several
weeks and sent them across the Atlantic. Sometimes
we forget that initial creativity that Bishop Dubuis and
Sr. Angelique had.*

*The other part that I love about Bishop Dubuis is
he didn't sit there and hold those first Sisters' hands.
Mother St. Pierre and Mother Madeleine had to figure it
out for themselves and get on with it, and they did. They
built relationships with the people of San Antonio. They
collaborated with the physicians in the city and then
learned how to be good nurses as a result. Immediately
they recognized the need for a nursing school. When
little children were being left on their doorstep someone
said, "We need an orphanage," and the community
joined with them to support it. Going toward the need
and meeting it—that is the radical phase.*

*We are grounded in our history because it projects
us into the future. The only way we can be radical
today is to be incarnate in the world. I have to be this
Incarnate Word. I have to look at Jesus and see how
He responded. He met every human being in his or her
social context, He engaged them in that context, and
only then was there the question or the issue of what
needed to be done. How we engage in these encounters
leads us to what needs are to be addressed. This journey
to the margins always must be grounded in prayer, in
the heart of God, because God then always reveals the*

*path. After the revelation, we have to be able to discern it, sift it out and see where it is taking us.*

For our Sisters, and for those who are serving with them, this path is out to the frontier, just as it was for two young Frenchwomen living under clear Texas skies 150 years ago.

The idea of being on the frontier appeals to me because the mission isn't static. The mission is alive. The mission is seeking out, finding a need, being a spark, and creating a community of others who share the vision.

The frontier is also closer to home in St. Louis, and it's that spirit of the frontier charism that had me seeking out a new path to address the racial disparities in home ownership. Traditionally, low and moderate housing took years to develop. Financing is the primary obstacle—government grants and tax credit programs can take years to access and come with numerous restrictions and red tape. Meanwhile boarded up buildings continue to deteriorate and the fabric of the neighborhood frays.

The need was there. It was time for the spark. I broached the idea with Archbishop Robert Carlson at one of our regular meetings. The next thing I knew, he was introducing me to someone at our annual grant reception by saying, "Bridget and I are going to be building some houses together."

Within a month, with a map of the Dutchtown neighborhood in tow, a small group of us met with the Archbishop and the idea that became the St. Joseph Housing Initiative quickly took fire. We looked past the obstacles and focused on the mission. The Archbishop gave us the green light to create a plan and six weeks later Mike England, the president of St. Mary's High School, Marie Kenyon, the director of the Archdiocesan Peace and Justice Commission and I were gathered around an antique table carved with a relief of the Last Supper to begin our presentation.

The Archbishop dispensed with our analysis, quickly went through the pages of the material, and said all he needed to know was how much it would cost. I said, "Two million." He said, "How about one?" Three years later, the St. Joseph Housing Initiative has renovated seven homes and counting. The first house that we rehabbed has a lunette window in the second story over the front porch. I had helped clean out that room and it was a charming dormer space that spanned the entire front of the home. A young girl in the family was talking to me at the house blessing and when I asked her which room was hers, she pointed at the window and said, "That's my room, and when it rains I am going to sit at the window and pretend I am in a castle."

Now I find myself driving down alleys and one-way streets in Dutchtown scouting out worn brick houses that can be rehabbed for families who want to build a new life for their family and make that vacant house a home once again. The day the Archbishop called to tell me that he had the start-up funds for the project he said, "You and

I see endless possibilities." Those endless possibilities are the frontier charism.

# Jubilee: Here I Am, Lord

The May temperatures were in the upper 80s as I left my room at the Generalate and walked across the Sisters' campus. Shiny long-tailed grackles foraged for insects under the old pecan trees on the lawn as I made my way to the Chapel and Jubilee, the day when our Sisters celebrate special anniversaries of their vows. I looked up at the trumpeting angels on the red brick corners of the green copper bell tower that had stood for more than 100 years, their horns held aloft. I walked up the flight of stone steps to the Romanesque archway and passed under the window above the heavy Chapel doors and its inscription captured in stained glass:

*Praised be the Incarnate Word.*

"Forever, Amen," I silently answered, as so many had before me.

I had been with the Sisters almost two decades and in my mind, they were a constant in a turbulent world. It was beginning to dawn on me, however, that they were changing, too. Sisters whom I had met in their 50s were now in their 70s. Sr. Dot and Sr. Neomi were gone, and so was Sr. Rosie. Discussions about what happens "when there were no Sisters" were occurring more frequently. Because the Sisters rarely retired, it was easy to delude myself into thinking there were 500 Sisters. In reality, even with a more robust vocation effort, the Sisters numbered slightly more than 250, and that number was decreasing each year.

The Chapel consecration occurred in 1907, a time of rapid Congregational expansion. Mother St. Pierre and Mother Madeleine had passed away and the next generation of leaders would oversee the rapid growth of the Congregation and its ministries. The Sisters had that in mind, and they built accordingly, with long rows of carved golden oak monastic stalls facing each other across the broad marble aisle that could accommodate 100s of Sisters. Those seats were only about one-third full today.

On this bright May morning, no one there was focused on mourning past glories or what some would say were the "halcyon decades of religious life." The Sisters were celebrating very much in the present. I was glad to be with so many friends, embraced by the love and care that renewed me every time I was with them in San Antonio. Sisters I barely knew made a point of happily reaching out to share how the Foundation was carrying out their mission and their joy in our common mission touched my heart.

The Chapel sparkled with the rainbow reflections of the stained-glass windows and cherubs balanced high over the ornate capitals of the rosy pillars that led to the sanctuary. As Mass began, I looked over pews of women, many now white-headed, and thought of all that they had accomplished.

The first reading, from the Book of Samuel centered on God's call:

> *The Lord called to Samuel, who answered,*
> *"Here I am." Samuel, 3:4*

The Jubilarians had answered that call, some for more than 75 years. They had come to this Chapel as young women—teenagers—and packed their trunk for the first assignment. They sailed through Vatican II and embraced change even when it turned their lives upside down, and when friends left while they stayed.

As the decades went by, they taught school, walked the halls of the hospitals caring for patients, worked as missionaries, and started new ministries at the time other people would typically retire.

What had it all meant and how did they see it continuing?

Sr. Tere Maya's reflection after the Gospel provided an answer to that question:

*Sister Jubilarians and friends, today we gather to CELEBRATE!*

*Our Jubilarians have come full circle this year of Jubilee: letting the land lie fallow, living into the freedom of God's call, working diligently for justice, healing division with reconciliation, and now celebrating God's steadfast love.*

*The call of the Lord to Samuel came at a time when 'the word of the Lord was scarce and vision infrequent.' It feels very much like our time when the word of God is 'scarce and vision infrequent' with volcanoes erupting, senseless shootings, and massive migrations. What a witness your lives bear at a time 'when vision is infrequent.' Your 25, 50, 60, or 75 years of steadfastness is undoubtedly the quiet voice of God speaking to our time, the vision of God lived out through each one of you in the everyday ministry of sharing the reign of God.*

*In many ways, we celebrate the journey from Samuel to Eli, the time from your first, 'Here I am,' to the call today to mentor the new Samuels among us. Even for our silver jubilarians, this is a new moment. Eli could not see, age had made him frail, and yet he had a critical mission, as you do. He was a faithful elder! His blindness made his hearing more acute. He knows what Samuel must do, and he is patient in explaining it to him.*

*Eli passes on the wisdom by teaching Samuel to discern. Eli knows that saying, 'Here I am,' is not enough, and he teaches Samuel to say, 'Speak, your servant is listening.' Eli teaches Samuel to practice discernment. Only wise elders can do that: teach us to listen. The wisdom is passed on and explained. This call, this journey, is about listening.*

*Our time needs mentors and teachers like you, Sister Jubilarians. It needs women of faith, wisdom women, who can mentor us to truly listen with our hearts, to listen into the heart of humanity during a time when our planet needs to listen into God's vision.*

*When I reflect on young Samuel, I can only imagine all of your years of responding to God's call. There is Samuel, both asleep and yet willing, his eagerness to be of service is amazing. The first time he heard his name, 'he ran,' the second time, 'he rose,' the third time he, 'got up and went to Eli.'*

*I think of each of you as young religious—willing, able, ready to 'jump out of bed,' eager to do God's will. Somehow, I have a feeling that you may not be jumping out of bed quite as fast, but we have seen the beautiful ways in which you remain alert to where God is calling you. The eagerness remains. I am certain you still have those long nights when you awake and go back to sleep, hearing God's whisper for what is coming next.*

*Over and over, year after year, of responding, 'Here I am,' brought you to this Jubilee. How many, 'Here I am's,' I wonder; how many times, after a sleepless night, did you finally say, 'Here I am.' Look what each one of your responses has done with your life—new ministries, new cities, new communities, and these people gathered here. Your 'Here I am' called each one of us today to celebrate with you.*

*In the second reading, Paul, in his letter to the Colossians, writes:*

*Therefore, God's chosen ones, holy and loved, put on heartfelt compassion, kindness, humility, gentleness, and patience, accepting one another and forgiving one another if anyone has a complaint against another.*
*Colossians 3:12-13*

*Paul writes that holiness, discipleship, our 'Here I am' can only happen in community. We can only 'put on heartfelt Compassion' in relation to a community. We can only be kind, and humble and gentle and patient with another. Jubilee is as much a celebration of God's steadfastness and of your faithfulness, as it is a celebration of the community's faithfulness to you.*

*Your 'Here I am' has been possible in this Congregation of the Sisters of Charity of the Incarnate Word, with those we serve, with those we accompany and who accompany us. That is why we celebrate with you. We can 'do everything in the name of the Lord Jesus' only in community, the community we call Church, the community you live with, the community in ministry, the community of humankind.*

*Following Jesus is never about us. Your lives have taught us what you have learned as disciples of Jesus, that this call is about others, about losing yourself in the other. We respond to a call, when like Samuel, we become 'servants who listen.' The Gospel is clear: 'whoever serves me' must be with Jesus, 'where I am.'*

*You, the Jubilarians, know where Jesus is. You have found Him in so many places, in so many incredible people, some of whom are here today, some who are present in the communion of saints, in the most poor and vulnerable, in those in need. You are the Jubilarians of the Vatican Council, the Jubilarians that brought us out, that called us to go forward, the Jubilarians 'en salida,' ready to find Jesus in the margins.*

*Sisters, you have produced much fruit because you have lost your life in service. You are servant leaders who have let go to serve and you have sacrificed in joy. Today we celebrate an incredible harvest, baskets full of fruit, lives touched, advocacy done, creation cared for. You have been the hands of Jesus, and responded with an on-going 'Here I am,' to the call our first Sisters received in a letter from Bishop Claude Marie Dubuis in the 1860s:*

*Our Lord Jesus Christ, suffering in the persons of a multitude of the sick and infirm of every kind, seeks relief at your hands.*

*Your hands have served, your response has brought us here in gratitude. Today, we 'honor you in God.'*

I left the Chapel that day with the certainty that willing hands would continue to serve a mission that speaks not just to the Sisters, but also to people who have encountered them. The Jubilarians' response to the mission met the dynamic changes of the 20th century. As Sr. Rose Ann McDonald, CCVI, had said to me once:

*The heart of the Blue Hole is deep. We hold the mission deep within us. With fewer vocations, we are called to share the mission with the laity. They will carry on the mission in response to our prophetic voice. We are the prophets, and that can be painful for us, but the mission will continue onward in new ways.*

The mission still calls. The mission elicits the response, "Here I am, Lord."

# 250 Bowls: Holding the Spirit

I was meandering across the Motherhouse grounds toward the new Heritage Center. The Sisters had finished gleaning the last of the pecans from the grounds and only a few smashed nutshells remained on the parking lot. As I stepped back on the sidewalk in the shadow of the chapel, I bumped into Sr. Mary Cecilia Henry, CCVI. She was one of the newest members of the Congregation, and about my age. Sr. Mary is a musician named after her two grandmothers. A San Antonio native with a frank and sensitive demeanor and sharp brown eyes, the Heritage Center was her new ministry. She was developing it into a resource that would not merely focus on the Sisters' past but be a catalyst to inspire the lay leaders of current and future ministries.

It was a tall order. The renovations for the Heritage Center had been a major undertaking as the Sisters sorted through artifacts as small as Bishop Dubuis' gloves and as large as a wall sized mosaic from the old provincial house chapel in St. Louis to create a context for the work that was being carried out today. That wasn't, however, why she was glad to see me.

Sr. Mary told me that she had had a brilliant idea the night before. She was on the committee preparing for the Congregational Assembly, a meeting that the Sisters held in between their General Chapter meeting which took place every four years. Two Assemblies would be held, one in San Antonio and one in Mexico City, and more than 200 Sisters would attend. The Assembly centered on spirituality and gave the Sisters an opportunity to talk as a group about issues that arose between General Chapter meetings.

As she reflected on the theme for the gathering, it suddenly came to her: Small pottery bowls. Specifically, small blue pottery bowls with a fish stamped into each one to symbolize what was in the hidden depths of each Sister. Sr. Mary was aware that I was a potter and disingenuously asked whether I knew someone in San Antonio who could make the bowls.

The answer was obvious.

I would make the bowls. It was the least I could do for the Sisters who had walked with me for more than 20 years. I did some quick calculations. I could throw about 50 bowls in less than two hours. Then came trimming, the bisque fire, glazing, and the glaze kiln. How hard could it be? I even had carved a fish stamp several years before. It was a sign.

I quickly agreed and Sr. Mary was overjoyed. I had a suspicion that she had hoped that I would volunteer given the look in her eye. Her excitement was contagious, and I agreed to make some samples that I would bring back in a few weeks.

Back at my studio I sorted through the shelves and found several different blue bowls. The glossy cobalt glaze seemed too uniform in color and was quite dark. The opal glaze caught my eye with its many variations on the same pot. Bright cornflower blue where thick, darker blue turning to iridescent green at times where thin or caught on a ridge. I knew it would be perfect. I threw a few additional samples. Wide-lipped bowls, straight-sided bowls, bowls with a bit of a curve, some with a firm foot at the base, others gently rounded. I packed them up and took them to San Antonio.

It is always a roll of the dice when you take on a commission. The client has a vision and you, as an artist, have a vision. Usually those visions don't intersect and that's when the negotiations begin. In this case, however, Sr. Mary was delighted. The color and the fish design were exactly what she had in mind. That was good news since the opal blue glaze was easy and consistent from firing to firing.

She selected a tea bowl with no foot and a rounded bottom, a simple form for me to throw and trim. Sr. Mary also quickly found uses for most of the sample bowls and plates I had brought. They would make great offertory vessels. The few that were left I gave to Sr. Mary Margaret Bright for her new room since she had recently retired to San Antonio. She has quite a collection of my pots.

Carondelet Pottery, my studio, is in a blue-collar neighborhood of modest brick shotgun homes in the oldest part of St. Louis. I had bought the building as a foreclosure and when I turned on the water, the PVC pipes burst. They had never been glued together—evidently, they were there simply for display. Water bubbled up through a circular crack in the cement basement floor—my own miniature Blue Hole. The plaster had seen better days and the tuck-pointing left much to the imagination. My husband and I worked together to rehab this three-room 19th century gem, although I think he would say "gem" was a bit of an overstatement. Now it was a functional studio with a sunny front room that housed my wheel, slab roller, and 1,000 pounds of porcelain.

I cracked open the box of white clay and hauled a 25-pound loaf over to the plaster wedging table, grabbed a wire, and sliced porcelain into one pound lumps that I weighed on the antique yellow kitchen scale. I rhythmically wedged each one a few times just to soften the edges and went to the wheel.

The porcelain hit the wheel head with a slap, and I began throwing bowls falling into a litany of centering, opening, and pulling. The white clay was soft and slick, and my fingers left rings on the exterior wall of the bowls as I pulled them to a somewhat consistent height, depth and width. As the wheel hummed and I threw, I thought of all the Sisters who would hold these bowls, offering prayers, looking into the depths for the fish, balancing the praying bowl in their hands. I thought of these women I had come to know, little kindnesses, encouragement and wisdom given to me freely. The bowls were a small gift compared to two decades of relationship.

I set the bowls to dry. They took over the shelving, covered the slab roller and invaded the gallery space, each stamped with a small leaping fish.

I spent the next afternoon trimming, placing each bowl upside down, centered on the wheel head. The sharp tools shaving the clay reminded me of making carrot curls with a potato peeler as long spirals of clay flew off the bowls one by one. As I trimmed, different bowls emerged. Some were perfectly round with a strong circle on the bottom. Others were a little wonky with a slight tilt. A few were not quite dry enough, but I trimmed them anyway and the chattering trimming tool left wavering rings where a perfect spiral might have appeared the next day. There were bowls for delicate hands and bowls that would be a comfortable fit for a larger palm. Bowls as individual as each Sister herself.

After a two-day candling of the kiln and then a quicker bisque firing, the bowls were ready to glaze. I dipped them into the green pickle bucket filled with lavender cream that would burst bright blue when fired to cone six.

As I unloaded the glaze kiln the variations of blue popped against the ivory kiln brick. The bowls were perfect. Lining them up on the table at first glance, they were a uniform Congregation. Under more intense scrutiny, individuality asserted itself.

That one was a little rounder. This one a bit taller. Then a shorter one, with more weight. The spiral on the bottom of another was almost invisible, but trimming ridges boldly crept up the side of the bowl to the right. In some a fish was clearly incised, while in others the fish was obscured by glaze. One or two held no fish at all. I hoped the fish-less bowls would not end up in the hands of Sisters who took the idea of the fish hiding in the depths too literally or they would spend a lot of time searching for what wasn't there.

I packed the bowls in bubble wrap. They would be taken to San Antonio and Mexico City via "Sister Mail," one of my favorite Congregational idiosyncrasies. Sisters transported letters, books and other items as part of their travel itinerary, similar to the owls dropping letters at Hogwarts, with the postage comprised of a scrawled, "through the kindness of," and the name of whatever Sister made the delivery, no stamps needed. Sr. Mary Cecilia was lining up willing couriers even as I packed the bowls.

I put the final blue bowl in the last brown box. In a few weeks, the Sisters would carefully select bowls that were far bluer than the bright aqua waters of the Blue Hole as they began their opening prayer ritual. They would each hold their bowl in the palm of prayer, perhaps catching an echo of my prayers that formed each bowl on the wheel.

Two hundred fifty Blue Hole wisdom bowls. Holding my spirit and theirs.

# Headwaters at Incarnate Word:
# A Location, A Mission, A State of Mind

### THE LOCATION

Headwaters at Incarnate Word stewards a 53-acre urban riparian forest known as the Headwaters Sanctuary. Centrally located along migratory corridors, this forest habitat supports a diverse wildlife population. The Sanctuary protects the Blue Hole or Yanaguana, "Mother Water", the source spring of the San Antonio River and a sacred fountain spring which once rose up to twenty feet in the air continuously. The four fountain springs along the Balcones Escarpment are thought to be depicted in Lower Pecos rock art, the White Shaman panel, which dates back 4,000 years. Archaeological finds in the Headwaters Sanctuary have provided evidence of human presence for approximately 12,000 years. Today, the Sanctuary is the only undeveloped parcel remaining from a 283-acre purchase made by the Sisters of Charity of the Incarnate Word from Colonel George Brackenridge in 1897. Headwaters at Incarnate Word Inc. and The Sisters of Charity of the Incarnate Word signed a conservation easement agreement with Green Spaces Alliance of South Texas on July 22, 2020 which protects the Sanctuary in perpetuity. The Headwaters Sanctuary and its Blue Hole continue to be a destination for indigenous peoples as well as tourists and San Antonians for its cultural, historical, geological, ecological, and spiritual value. Headwaters at Incarnate Word is the only nature sanctuary in the heart of San Antonio.

THE MISSION

Our mission is to preserve, restore, and celebrate the rich natural, cultural, historical, spiritual, and educational values of the headwaters of the San Antonio River, especially within the 53-acre Headwaters Sanctuary. We respond to the call for a sustainable relationship with God's creation by offering environmental education, reflective experiences on care of creation, and practical, hands-on volunteer opportunities to restore and protect the land. Headwaters at Incarnate Word is a nonprofit sponsored Earth care ministry of the Sisters of Charity of the Incarnate Word.

A STATE OF MIND

The San Antonio Spring, also called the Blue Hole, is a famous artesian spring on the Congregational heritage land of the Sisters of Charity of the Incarnate Word. Indigenous peoples here at the time of colonization called the springs Yanaguana, or "Mother Water". Coahuiltecan Native American creation stories describe how the Spirit Waters rose up, giving birth to all Creation.

"The whole river gushes up in one sparkling burst from the earth …The effect is overpowering. It is beyond your possible conceptions of a spring." (Frederick Law Olmstead, landscape architect and designer of New York's Central Park, 1857)

This great spring was once a fountain spring rising up to twenty feet in the air. It joins Comal Springs, San Marcos Springs, and Barton Springs as one of the four fountain springs of Texas. Indeed, there is evidence to suggest these same four fountain springs may be depicted in a rock wall painting, known as the White Shaman Panel in the Lower Pecos, dating back some 4,000 years ago.

These four great springs issue from a common water source, the vast Edwards Aquifer that flows underground along the Balcones Escarpment from west of Del Rio to north of Austin. The springs give rise to life-giving rivers that have sustained human communities for thousands of years. Evidence of human presence in the headwaters of these rivers dates back nearly 12,000 years, signifying the importance of these great springs to early human civilization.

The San Antonio Springs were understood to be the source of the San Antonio River: "The key to the situation, the Ojo de Agua, the birthright of the city" (William Corner, 1890).

Now the population of San Antonio is well over a million, all dependent on water from the Edwards Aquifer, which is riddled with many artesian wells. The first artesian wells drilled into the Edwards Aquifer in the 1890s had the immediate effect of reducing spring flow. Increased pumping to supply water to an expanding population has caused further drawdown of the aquifer, leaving local springs dry much of the time.

The headwaters remain a powerful symbol of the literal and spiritual life-giving essence of water. Flowing or not, they remain, to many, the sacred springs.

HEADWATERS AT INCARNATE WORD
Headwaters-iw.org

*Photo by Gregg Eckhardt*

# Acknowledgments

When I set off to write a book more than a decade ago. I had absolutely no idea how long of a journey it would be. Sprints, not marathons, are much more my style. So many people helped me get to the finish line, and then pulled me across it at the end of the road.

Wonderful people provided encouragement along the way. My husband, Michael, found subtle and not so subtle ways to encourage me to write, and at times with no complaint let me take over the dining room table, the library table, and even the windowsills, with all of my materials and files. He was also on call to find lost charger cords and my missing cellphone. My daughter, Amelia, was a fantastic – and patient – editor, and my daughter, Carolyn, created an amazing painting for the cover and managed to take a photo of me that makes me look much wiser than I actually am.

I appreciate my staff at the Foundation, particularly Marty Glosemeyer and Lisa Durham, for their help with all of the details of organizing a book, Maria Rodgers O'Rourke for editorial advice, Mike Fitzgerald for his encouragement, and Sr. Helena Monahan, CCVI, for her wisdom. Sr. Helena and Sr. Theresa McGrath, CCVI, were instrumental in identifying the corrections and final edits to the book.

My friends also played a key role. I can't imagine having to transcribe hours of interviews, but my friends Pat Thibodeau and Laura Hawes both stepped up. Without them, the book would have taken another decade. I appreciate my traveling companions, Lisa Uribe, Ana De-Hoyos O'Connor, and Cynthia Aguirre. And I am grateful for all the friends who dropped an encouraging word along the way. Each time that happened, I took it as a sign to continue.

I am thankful for my circle of writing coaches and friends, Christina Baldwin of PeerSpirit, and Lynn Fena, Janis Hall, Sara Harris, Taline Manassian, Pamela Sampel, and Gretchen Staebler, among others, for time spent together writing on Whidbey Island, and in Winona, Wheatland, and Dripping Springs. I am also grateful for the late Sr. Mary Ann Eckhoff, SSND, who was the best mentor anyone could have ever had.

I want to thank Cathy Davis and her staff at Davis Creative for the project management and book design; Wendy Barnes for a beautiful book cover design as well

## Acknowledgments

as ideas on marketing and promotion; Suann Fields for technical advice; and Marstin Digital Services Ltd. for the Incarnate Word Foundation Press website design.

I am indebted to Martha Quiroga for facilitating the Spanish translation of the manuscript, to Catalina Johnson for editing the Spanish translation, and to Sr. Maria Luisa Vélez Garcia, CCVI, for her edit and review of the translation.

I would be remiss if I did not acknowledge the value of *Promises to Keep: A History of the Sisters of Charity of the Incarnate Word, San Antonio, Texas* by Sr. Margaret Patrice Slattery, CCVI, as well as the assistance of Donna Morales Guerra, Director of Archives and Record Management for the Congregation.

Finally, I have heartfelt gratitude to the Incarnate Word Sisters for all the wisdom they have shared with me over the years. Being with them has changed my life in so many ways. They shared a plethora of stories, only a fraction of which I could include in this book, and I hold all those stories in my heart.

# About the Author

Bridget McDermott Flood is the Executive Director of the Incarnate Word Foundation, a ministry of the Sisters of Charity of the Incarnate Word, San Antonio, where she manages the Foundation's grant making and community initiatives. Nationally, Bridget served on the White House Task Force for Reform of the Faith and Neighborhood-Based Office under the Obama Administration. She serves on the Boards of NETWORK Lobby for Social Justice, the Headwaters at Incarnate Word, FADICA, and the

St. Joseph Housing Initiative. Bridget graduated from Saint Louis University with a bachelor's degree in English and political science, and a master's degree in urban affairs.

She is also an artist at her studio, Carondelet Pottery, and is a beekeeper. Bridget lives with her husband, Michael, in St. Louis. She and her husband have two daughters, Amelia and Carolyn, and two grandsons.

Bridget is the author of a spirituality blog, www.blueholewisdom.com. To contact Bridget, email bridget.flood@iwfdn.org or blueholewisdom@gmail.com